Truancy Revisited

Students as School Consumers

Rita E. Guare
Bruce S. Cooper

A Scarecrow Education Book

The Scarecrow Press, Inc.
Lanham, Maryland, and Oxford
2003

A SCARECROWEDUCATION BOOK

Published in the United States of America
by Scarecrow Press, Inc.
A Member of the Rowman & Littlefield Publishing Group
4501 Forbes Boulevard, Suite 200, Lanham, Maryland 20706
www.scarecroweducation.com

PO Box 317
Oxford
OX2 9RU, UK

British Library Cataloguing in Publication Information Available

Library of Congress Cataloging-in-Publication Data
Guare, Rita E., 1949–
  Truancy revisited : students as school consumers / Rita E. Guare, Bruce S.
Cooper.
    p. cm.
"A ScarecrowEducation book."
Includes bibliographical references and index.
  ISBN 0-8108-4553-9 (hardcover : alk. paper) — ISBN 0-8108-4554-7
(pbk. : alk. paper)
  1. School attendance—United States. I. Cooper, Bruce S. II. Title.
  LB3081 .G89 2003
  371.2'9'0973—dc21   2002011768

∞™ The paper used in this publication meets the minimum requirements of
American National Standard for Information Sciences—Permanence of Paper
for Printed Library Materials, ANSI/NISO Z39.48-1992.
Manufactured in the United States of America.

Contents

List of Figures and Tables   v

Foreword   ix

1   Truancy Revisited: From a Student Deficit Model to
        Rational Choice Theory   1

2   Truancy Analyzed: The Students' View   17

3   Fighting Truancy: A Three-Pronged Approach   73

Appendix: Student Truancy & Attendance Review (STAR-II)   87

References   93

Index   97

About the Authors   101

List of Figures and Tables

Figure

2.1   Structure of this Study, as Applied to School (Blanket) and
      Classroom (Post-Registration) Truancy   23

Table

1.1   NELS:88 2nd Follow-Up Survey of Class Truancy,
      Seniors: 1992, Still in School   5
1.2   NELS:88 2nd Follow-Up Survey of School Truancy,
      Seniors: 1992, Still in School   6
1.3   Truancy from Classes for NELS:88, Sample Student
      "Drop-Outs"   6
2.1   Characteristics of Sample Students   20
2.2   Age Distribution and After-School Work of
      Sample Students   21
2.3   Sample School Characteristics   21
2.4   Comparison of Truancy: School v. Class   24
2.5   School Truancy by Building Site   24
2.6   Cutting Class by Building Site   25
2.7   Cutting Class: Comparing Male and Female
      Student Behavior   27
2.8   School Truancy by Gender   29

2.9 Cutting Behavior of Male and Female Pupils:
Cutting To Where? 30
2.10 Cutting Class: Alone or "With Friends" by Gender 30
2.11 Cutting School with Whom? By Gender (Blanket Truancy) 31
2.12 Rates of Getting Caught Cutting Class by Gender 32
2.13 Rates of Getting Caught Cutting School by Gender 33
2.14 School Notifying Home for Cutting Class by Gender 34
2.15 School Notifying Home for Student "Blanket" Truancy
(Skipping School) by Gender 34
2.16 Being Punished for "Blanket" Truancy (Skipping School)
by Gender 35
2.17 Being Punished for "Post-Registration" Truancy
(Skipping Class) by Gender 36
2.18 School Truancy by Ethnic Group 37
2.19 Truancy from Classes (Post-Registration) by Ethnic Group 38
2.20 Truancy from School by Levels of English Spoken in
the Home 39
2.21 Incidence of Students Cutting Class by "Pretending"
to Need Help Falsely—by Ethnic Group 40
2.22 Cutting Class and Staying on School Property
by Ethnicity 41
2.23 Cutting School with Whom? by Ethnic Group 42
2.24 Cutting Class with Whom? by Ethnic Group 42
2.25 Classroom Truancy and Frequency of Students'
"Getting Caught" 43
2.26 Reported School Truancy to the Home by
Ethnic/Racial Group 45
2.27 School Punishment Rates for Cutting Classes
by Ethnic Group 46
2.28 Cutting Class Segmented by Students'
Self-Reported Grades 47
2.29 School Truancy by Achievement Level 48
2.30 Cutting Class "to Where?" By Students'
Self-Reported Grades 49
2.31 Punishment for Cutting Class by Academic
Achievement Level 50

2.32 Truancy from Class by Students' Grade Level, 8th–12th   52
2.33 Cutting School by Years in School   53
2.34 School Truancy by Grade Level   54
2.35 Location of Cutting Classes by Grade Level   55
2.36 Cutting Class—Pretending to Need Help by Grade Level   56
2.37 Frequency of Students Cutting Class and Getting Caught
       by Grade Level   56
2.38 "Telling Parents" about Cutting School by Grade Level   58
2.39 Being Punished for Cutting Class by Grade Level   59
2.40 Truancy Rules as Understood by Students   60
2.41 School Truancy by Students' Willingness to Recommend
       Their School to Friends ("Satisfaction" Measure)   62
2.42 Reliability Measures for Eight STAR Sub-Scales   65
2.43 Correlation of Cutting School and Class with
       Student Attitudes   66
2.44 Multiple Regression Analysis of Truancy and Student
       Attitudes, Characteristics, and School Descriptors   69
2.45 Multiple Regression Analysis of Student Attitudes,
       Academic Progress, and Student Satisfaction   70

Foreword

TRUANCY AS A RATIONAL CHOICE

Writing *Winning the Brain Race* with David T. Kearns in the late 1980s (when he was still chairman and CEO of Xerox), we advanced a novel argument about the identity of a corporation's most important customer. It was neither the customer who returned year after year without complaint nor the customer who complained and still returned (he or she, after all, offered constructive criticism); the most important customer was the one who abandoned you and never told you why. Without knowing what you had done to forfeit a customer's loyalty, we argued, you, the manager, were virtually helpless. You could not make the changes in goods or services necessary to regain that customer's trust and build your customer base. And to find out what was going on, the firm had to find the drop-out and find out why brand loyalty had evaporated.

We meant by this to offer a principled example of a business practice that had a bearing on schools. Our effort was predicated on the fact that the business community was becoming apoplectic about the quality of the nation's schools, and not just because *A Nation at Risk* (1983) had just been released. Business leaders were informed by their own sources, both at home and abroad. In the case of Xerox, the Japanese were eating our lunch, because, among other things, they had the best-prepared workforce in the world. They needed virtually no on-the-job training and no on-the-job education at all. As Kearns famously said about American business and the schools, "If the schools educate, business will train." And for those readers who missed the point, we stated it as baldly as we could. The customer "drop-out" was precisely analogous to the school drop-out. And the school should be as worried about its drop-outs as business is about its drop-outs.

As this splendid short book—*Truancy Revisited*—makes clear, it has taken nearly two decades for someone in the field of education to take this truism to heart. If there are truants and drop-outs there are reasons, and the first place to begin inquiring about it is among the truants themselves, the students. As Rita E. Guare and Bruce S. Cooper so ably chronicle, there is a good deal to be learned from such students. Perhaps the most important lesson is to treat them as consumers who are making a rational choice. There is method to pupils' apparent madness.

Indeed, only in a monopoly system, which to add insult to injury, requires compulsory attendance (a sort of monopoly squared), could the issue be framed in the terms it has been historically. To wit, everything is right with the schools, thank you very much; it's those dreadful truants who are the problem. In this connection, one must be forgiven for remembering the late and unlamented former governor of Georgia, Lester Maddox, who, complaining about the state of his prisons observed that they couldn't be improved until Georgia "got a better class of prisoner." Sound familiar?

At a somewhat more elevated level, one is reminded of Ted Sizer's fictional Horace (of *Horace's Compromise*). A master teacher of no small accomplishment, because Horace was nonetheless not a magician, he had no magic wand to wave to keep the attention of all his students. The deal Horace struck was straightforward and sensible: if bored students didn't bother him, Horace would return the favor. The book struck such a resonant cord with me that for a while I actually thought that Ted Sizer had heard about my modern European history high school teacher, Mr. Dean. Not only did Mr. Dean love modern European history, he carefully scavenged covers and bound signature copies of the great Carl Becker's high school history text for us to tape together to make whole books. (The Chicago Board of Education, in its wisdom, didn't bother to issue new textbooks when the old ones wore out.) To be precise, the ten or twelve of us who wanted to learn something taped together a dog-eared copy of the Becker book; the remaining dozen students slept in the back of the room where they didn't need lectures or books. Mr. Dean, a man of his word, had promised them each a "D" if they kept quiet. They did and he did.

Then there is the category of students that former Charlotte-Mecklenburg School District Superintendent John Murphy has identified with professional detachment and scientific precision: *MLB's* is his acronym of choice ("mean little bastards," for the uninitiated). These are the kids that most teachers are thrilled to see drop out, or at least be truant on a regular basis. And so it goes.

There is a wealth of information for the interested reader in Guare and Cooper's book, and each reader will have his or her favorite illustrations. Among the wonderful variety of tables my favorite is table 2.25, *Classroom Truancy and Frequency of Getting "Caught."* The text accompanying it dryly observes that of the ethnic groups "Latinos/ Latinas were most skillful at cutting and not getting caught, with their average NOT CAUGHT running 71.0 percent." By way of contrast 53.3 percent of African Americans were not caught and Whites were really out of luck: precisely half got caught, an inauspicious beginning to be sure. (My closest friend in high school was a truancy genius; the first time he was really sick he got a note from his mother—which was to be signed by every single teacher whose class he had missed. He promptly tore it up and forged one in motherly handwriting; if someone suspected him of cutting class and called home, his mother would unwittingly give him a perfect alibi. As I remember he was never caught in four years. He should have gone into the CIA when he grew up, but instead became a jazz percussionist.)

Indeed, in this comprehensive, thorough and thoughtful book, only one thing is missing: a commentary on the ideas of Rutgers Professor Jackson Toby and me (so far as I know we are the only two education analysts seriously to advance the radical idea that compulsory attendance should be abolished altogether). I know of Professor Toby only through the printed word so I shall not speak for him, but I do commend his work to the interested reader. (At age 75 he has taken the year off, with what is probably the longest teaching tenure—50 years—in the history of Rutgers; maybe in the history of higher education.)

In my case, upon the reissuance of *Winning the Brain Race* three years after its initial release, I had the opportunity to edit, nay, rewrite, the opening chapter and my publisher gave me carte blanche. In the revised and updated version, then, appears my most radical recommendation: eliminate compulsory attendance altogether (I quailed and suggested that age

14 was the right point to abandon it), and replace it with what I called *guaranteed access*. Access to what, one might ask: to a high quality program of academic instruction that would accept you no matter what your age, appearance or disposition so long as you were willing to work and work hard. And that—hard work by students—is surely the secret weapon in high performing schools. It certainly explains the differences in performance across cultures.

In closing, I had hoped that the recommendation would be taken seriously because compulsion and education are fundamentally incompatible. Indeed, the one justification for compulsory attendance that rings true is the state's interest is sparing children from economic serfdom, from parents who would thrust a child into the workplace at the expense of their long-term health and welfare, which is to say, their education. And the expense is great—recent census data make the point powerfully, revealing that education pays and pays handsomely. As Harvard President Derek Bok is reported to have said, "If you think education is expensive try ignorance." In today's global economy to choose not to be educated has one description only: irrational choice. Truancy and dropping out are rational choices in the context of contemporary school organization; the signal they send is that schools should pull up their socks.

Finally Guare and Cooper are right to offer a menu of policy prescriptions to address the questions raised by truancy; in particular, framing the issue in terms of rational choice theory puts the argument where it belongs, in the tradition of reasoned discourse not polemical breast-beating.

And as I wrote more than a decade ago I would write again today: compulsory attendance should be abandoned not because school is unimportant but precisely because it is so important. Guare and Cooper have made a thoughtful contribution to this important discussion by going straight to the source: the students themselves, and by so doing, illuminating a subject too often characterized by more heat than light.

Denis P. Doyle
Chevy Chase, MD
August 5, 2002

1

Truancy Revisited: From a Student Deficit Model to Rational Choice Theory

We real cool. We left school.
We lurk late. We strike straight.
We sing sin. We thin gin.
We jazz June. We die soon.

Poet Gwendolyn Brooks

INTRODUCTION

Truancy goes by many names—unexcused absences, absenteeism, student "indiscipline," and "early school leaving"—and has many attributed causes including personal deficits, peer group pressures, school-specific problems, and even societal shortcomings. It apparently can have serious effects on students and society, leading to the interruption and deterioration of learning, academic failure, school drop-out, and "the loss of credentials which are necessary for future success" (Birman & Natriello, 1978, p. 31).

Yet, for all its seriousness, effects, and implications, few researchers have consulted with students about their own truancy, their recall of the consequences of being absent without an excuse, and the relationship between students' perceptions of their school and their truancy. And we know that schools are notoriously bad at gathering and reporting accurate data on truancy; officials, we believe, underestimate, and more importantly, inaccurately report the extent of the problem.

This study seeks to correct this oversight. We surveyed students, asking them how often they skipped school and cut class. And, as was the case in a parallel study in England (Stoll & O'Keeffe, 1989), truancy of both sorts (absence from school and from classes after being marked "present" at school) was far higher than the "official" levels: 38.9 percent skipped school without an excuse and a full 69 percent cut classes.

The best data we have on truancy today are patchy and inconclusive, not that this study is a national sample. We preferred to explore a few hundred students' behaviors, motives, and consequences in depth, exploiting the impersonality (and thus, the confidentiality) of an instrument that bore no threat or consequence for students—while a personal interview might have frightened students away, forcing them to admit verbally their illegal actions.

Using a new instrument, the *Student Truancy and Attendance Review-II* (STAR), we heard from students themselves: how often they cut, with whom, where they went when they "disappeared," their rate of getting caught, how often contacts were made by school officials with the home to report their absences, and their punishment (if any and what). Hence, this study fills a serious void in the vast literature on truancy: it attempts to dispel several misconceptions about the nature of truancy.

First, we reject the rather simplistic view that truancy is the result of a personal deficit or characteristic of students; second, we also have reservations about the view that students skip out mainly because their friends do it. And third, schools and society, while partially to blame, cannot be the whole story. What emerges from this analysis is yet another view: one that treats students as thinking, rational decision makers who assess their situation and decide, like other "consumers" or "clients," to "buy" their units of education (a day or a period at a time) or to reject school and play hooky.

While some chronic cutters are undoubtedly troubled youth who cannot "fit into the system"; and while the power of the kid culture is often powerful for school-age children; and while schools and society may be generally unaware of just how boring, tedious, unchallenging and unrewarding some schooling must be, we found evidence that truancy is so widespread—across the sexes, the age cohorts, the grade levels, and the ethnic groups—that deficit, social, and school theories cannot explain adequately the root causes of truancy.

Adult researchers, then, have underestimated the ability of young people to "read" the mandatory system of education, to calculate the risks of getting caught, having their parents informed, and failing their work, when deciding when and where to be truant. Furthermore, as Natriello (1990) and others have argued, absenteeism is not a single problem; rather it's a highly complex interaction among student, school, and classroom variables that all influence the students' decision-making processes. The determination to attend or be absent, we found, is systematically influenced by students' perceptions of home, teacher, school, and self. Thus, like any decision maker, students exhibit "limited" or "bounded rationality" when making a choice to attend or not to attend a particular class or school day.

Thus, since some rational calculations are made, students are open to influences to attend more frequently or not to be truant at all. We have data to suggest that schools and districts do a poor job of delineating the rules on student absences, explaining them, and enforcing them. Again, with a dearth of clear rules and expectations, students apparently do the "rational" thing: they fiddle with the system, cutting and skipping. What may then appear as inappropriate, deleterious, and even irrational behavior to researchers from outside the students' heads and the schools' walls, is imperfectly reasonable if we consider the personal, social, and rational explanations for truant actions.

At the point where school and researchers cease to "blame the victim," and stop excusing the actions because students are disturbed, deprived, and deficient, we begin to get a clearer picture of truancy. And with a fresh view, schools can begin to see their students as "clients" and "consumers" of education, not just as delinquents. For while heavy enforcement of truancy requirements has a short-term effect (Wilson, 1993), it should be coupled with greater enticements for students to attend school. Making classrooms a more fulfilling place, making school an experience worthy of the thousands of hours and dollars invested in each pupil each year, and creating opportunities for students to get jobs—making an education "worth" it—all combine to reduce absenteeism and to increase student learning and development time in school.

Chapter 1

THE LITERATURE

A vast literature exists on truancy. A trip to the Web produced 702 sources through a single search. And the discussion of the topic is hardly consistent. Studies dating back to the 1970s were both empirical (data based) and more theoretical and philosophical, with statistical studies using "missing school" (absenteeism), for whatever reason, as a key predictor of student success in school and beyond.

For example, Moos and Moos (1978) related "classroom climate" to students' absences, which in turn predicted pupil grades. These authors wrote: "The absenteeism rate is a particularly important intermediate outcome variable, since students are less likely to be affected by classrooms that they attend less frequently" (p. 264). The findings, first, showed "the rank order correlation between absenteeism and grades was −.45, indicating a tendency for student absences to be higher in classes with more stringent grading practices" (p. 265).

Or, do more rigorous teachers present materials and concepts that nonattending students cannot catch up on and learn? As in most correlation studies, it is difficult to tell which way the relationship or causality is running: Do stringent teachers with high standards drive students away, as Moos and Moos contend? Or are students who are absent simply unable to master work in high-level learning environments and thus the relationship between truancy and achievement is negative?

Second, when absenteeism is correlated with the "classroom environment," item by item, the authors found that "controlling" teachers had higher absence rates than "involving" teachers, as Moos and Moos determined:

> Students in classes with *high absenteeism rates* are more likely to feel that they are often watching the clock, that they need to be careful about what they say, that there are clear and set rules, and that it is relatively easy to get into trouble in the class. These students are also more likely to state that they do not enjoy the class, that they cannot discuss outside activities in class, that passing the class is relatively difficult, and that the teacher is fairly strict. (1978, p. 265)

The results of the Moos and Moos study are interesting. The findings are based on a small sample of only nine classrooms (nine teachers), however.

And the authors correlated each item with absences, rather than creating subscales. Thus, in all, the study shows the importance of school attendance but fails to analyze why students were absent: Were they "truant" in the legal sense? Or were they sickly and were absent with a bonafide excuse.

The National Educational Longitudinal Studies-1988 (NELS:88), one of the largest samples of student behavior, surveyed over sixteen thousand students randomly selected from across the United States during their high school careers, a sample extended through the use of "weighting" to over 2.69 million students nationwide. NELS:88 traced these students from their eighth-grade year (1988) through high school (seniors in 1992) and beyond, even locating students who had dropped out of high school.

Table 1.1 shows both the unweighted and weighted levels and rates of cutting/skipping classes for those seniors still in school. These data show that 51 percent of the seniors admitted to having cut class at least once or twice during their school years. About a quarter of the group skipped at least three times or more.

Table 1.2 shows the same information for school cutting, which appears to be considerably higher in the NELS:88 sample. For example, data on skipping school show that 90.9 percent of the unweighted sample cut school at least once while the weighted sample of 2.6 million students or 91.5 percent admitted being truant from school. Hence, class truancy ran around 50 percent while missing school altogether was above 90 percent.

A third NELS:88 sample was taken of students who had *dropped out of high school* between the eighth-grade (1988) and twelfth grade (in 1992).

Table 1.1.   NELS:88 2nd Follow-Up Survey of Class Truancy, Seniors: 1992, Still in School "How many times did respondents cut classes?"

Cut Class	Unweighted Frequency	Unweighted Percent	Weighted Frequency	Weighted Percent
"Never" Truant	8,286	49.2	1,313,929	48.5
Truant:				
1–2 Times	4,248	25.2	702,205	25.9
3–6 Times	2,239	13.3	353,972	13.1
7–9 Times	851	5.1	133,811	4.9
10–15 Times	513	3.0	83,916	3.1
Over 15 times	714	4.2	120,166	4.4
Total Sample	16,851	100.0	2,707,999	100.0
Total Truants	8,565	50.8	1,394,070	51.48

Table 1.2.   NELS:88 2nd Follow-Up Survey of School Truancy, Seniors: 1992, Still in School "How many times did respondents cut school?"

Cut School	Unweighted Frequency	Unweighted Percent	Weighted Frequency	Weighted Percent
Never Truant	1,531	9.1	229,192	8.5
Truant:				
1–2 Times	5,124	26.9	932,129	34.6
3–6 Times	5,710	10.5	358,561	13.3
7–9 Times	2,219	5.7	206,684	7.7
10–15 Times	1,204	3.0	83,916	3.1
Over 15 Times	976	4.6	164,768	6.1
Total Sample	16,764	100.0	2,696,536	100.0
Total Truants	15,233	90.9	2,467,344	91.5

Data on this smaller sample of students cutting classes showed a higher level than the population still in school. That is, while 48.5 percent of the in-school students "Never" cut school, the drop-outs showed 34.1 percent "Never" cutting class. Hence, 65.9 percent cut class among the drop-outs while 51.48 percent of the in-school respondents admitted being truant from classes. See table 1.3.

These NELS:88 data show much higher levels of cutting school than we found, even though ours (see chapter two) found over two-thirds of the students cutting class, compared to 50 percent in the NELS:88 data. Whichever sample one consults, however, the rate of truancy seems excessively high at 90 percent missing school in NELS:88 and 67 percent cutting classes in this study (as well as the British survey by Stoll and O'Keeffe, 1989).

Table 1.3.   Truancy from Classes for NELS:88, Sample Student "Drop-Outs"

Cut Class	Unweighted Frequency	Unweighted Percent	Weighted Frequency	Weighted Percent
Never Truant	214	23.4%	59,578	34.1%
Truant:				
1–2 Times	126	13.8	28,629	16.4
3–6 Times	103	11.3	24,036	13.8
7–9 Times	34	3.7	7,181	4.1
10-plus Times	161	17.6	55,133	31.6
Total Truants	424	66.5%	114,979	65.9%
Total Sample	638	100.0%	174,557	100.0%

Two recent studies of achievement and student self-esteem, where attendance and truancy are intervening variables, were conducted by Liu, Kaplan, and Risser (1992) and Haller (1992). These authors, like Moos and Moos, built an explanatory model that predicted levels of student achievement based on their sense of self-efficacy, teacher responsiveness, stress, and motivation, as mediated by illness and absences. Liu and colleagues concluded: "Furthermore, general self-esteem, via its inverse effects on deviance and psychological distress, and the effects of these variables on illness, influences *absence from school and, therefore, academic achievement*" (1992, p. 137). Note the key linking role of being absent from school, between students' psychological standing and their grades in school.

Haller (1992) was attempting to relate school ruralness and size to key "indisciplines," including cutting school and class. He gathered data on both pupils' and principals' perceptions of the problems of truancy in their schools. He found that controlling for size and location explained a significant part of the variation in all the dependent variables. But smallness turned out to be a more important quality than ruralness. Thus, attendance continues to be a key variable in empirical studies, both as an outcome and a cause.

Other social scientists have treated school non-attendance from a more philosophical perspective. They use school absences as symbolic proxy somehow for deeper social and economic problems and go so far as to argue that "schools are structured to *discourage* attendance among certain groups of students and that absenteeism rates are a function of society's rate of unemployment" (Natriello, 1994, p. 34; emphasis added).

Suggested here is that some schools are actually organized to *cause* truancy among the poor and children of color, as a form of "practice" for life on the margins of unemployment, poverty, welfare, and participation in society among the disenfranchised. Thus, Carnoy and Levin (1976) believe that truancy and drop-out "legitimate the existing social order and lower levels of social mobility among some groups" (Natriello, 1994, p. 103; also see Carnoy & Levin, 1976).

Truancy has a legal context as well: it can be defined as student absences from school for officially unacceptable, unexcused (illegal) reasons—and has thus been a problem in formal education since school attendance became mandatory in the early twentieth century (Howard, Haynes & Atkinson, 1986; Hofkins, 1994; Zuckerman, 1984). Since an unexcused absence from school is a legal offense, these compulsory attendance laws, in Kaeser's words, "make educators agents of the legal system. Laws give school personnel responsibility and authority to intervene when children are absent" (Kaeser, 1991, p. 5199).

Birman and Natriello (1978) have noted the difference between requiring attendance at the elementary school level, which dates back to the 1920s in many states, and the more recent stipulation that high school students attend until their sixteenth or seventeenth birthdays:

> From an historical perspective, the problem of high school absenteeism [note they did not mention *truancy*] is only as old as compulsory attendance laws. Only when school attendance is mandated does non-attendance [truancy] become a crime. Only when school attendance becomes universal is non-attendance [truancy] viewed as deviant. In fact, there is some historical evidence which suggests that compulsory education laws were passed only after high school attendance was relatively widespread. . . . it is easy sometimes to forget that only in the past 25 years have high schools been attended by more than 50 percent of adolescence. (Birman & Natriello, 1978, p. 30)

Truancy can thus be differentiated from an "excused absence" for reasons of illness, religious observance, or other "legal" reasons that are acceptable to both parents and authorities at school (e.g., going to visit a college for possible application, traveling to an inter-school debate, or receiving medical help). The *International Encyclopedia of Education* (1994) explained the relationship between requiring an education for ten to twelve years and the rise of truancy: "One important reason that compulsory attendance laws are adopted is that they express public consensus about the value of education. Education is thought to be important as a source of individual growth and development, a key to effective and informed citizenship, an access route to better jobs and upward mobility, and crucial to a healthy economy" (Kaesar, 1991, p. 5298).

Furthermore, truancy (unlike absenteeism) involves an *unjustified* absence in which students themselves are the cause. Hence, technically students are not truant if their parents or guardians keep them home for various reasons. Here the parent is to blame and may be culpable under mandatory attendance laws; but the student is not expected to disobey a parent in order to attend school.

Truancy may, in fact, be a more serious condition than previously reported since a number of students are "officially present" (Stoll & O'Keeffe, 1989)—having been marked "in attendance" at the start of the day—but who then cut classes and may not be counted on records of school absenteeism rates. Called "post-registration truancy" in England (Stoll & O'Keeffe, 1989), this study alerted educators to the seriousness of the problem and the need for better data gathering and analysis.

In the United States of America until quite recently, truancy was defined as being absent from school completely, not missing classes. Jane Stallings, in her 1979 study, explains that the path to truancy starts with class cutting, not that being *absent from class is itself a form of truancy.* In her research on truancy in high school reading classes, she discovered that students were selective about cutting, not because of the teachers' personality but because of classroom practices. In classes with high cutting, students were more often assigned large quantities of written "seat work" and independent silent reading. In contrast, classes were better attended when they were characterized as more interactive and engaging. Stalling found, then, that class cutting is not simply a problem of adolescents with deficiencies but with classroom pedagogy that does not connect and involve students.

Importantly, "cutting" and "skipping" (called "bunking off" in Britain)— to use common student parlance—have often been associated with ill-performing schools, poor pupil achievement, and ultimately academic failure and drop-out (Reynolds & Murgatroyd, 1977). As such, truancy of all kinds is a major problem for students, teachers, and schools alike. For students, missing school can lead to a disconnection among the curriculum, learning and teaching, and difficulties in keeping up with lessons and assignments. Excessive truancy, however defined, often means failure, retention or repeating a grade, and eventually dropping out. For teachers, truant pupils may force the reteaching of classes, the need to repeat testing for students, and frustration with class progress—slowing the learning for those pupils who regularly attend and want to achieve.

And for schools, failure to attend may mean loss of revenues (as state aid per pupil is allocated based on "average daily attendance" or ADA in many systems), poor school performance, and loss of reputation and face in the community. With states increasingly "grading" schools on the overall performance of pupils (school "report cards" are now being issued in many places), high truancy levels can be an alarm signal for other, deeper curricular, staffing, and leadership problems.

Furthermore, in some cities, truancy can be bad for students' health— even life-threatening. One example: a headline, "4 Students Shot Near a School in Brooklyn," in the *New York Times* announced a fight and multiple shooting that started "over a basketball game between two groups of students . . . who were *not in class at the time*" (Jones, January 9, 1996, p. B1; emphases added). The shooting occurred at 1:15 PM in a park near George W. Wingate High School but involved students from both Wingate and South Shore High School two miles away.

New York City Schools chancellor, Dr. Rudy Crew, rushed to the hospital to visit the wounded young people, noting "that the shooting did not occur on the school's campus." Oddly enough, for some reason, the chancellor neglected to ask why these students were not in their appointed schools and classes under appropriate adult supervision. Were any of these victims (or gunmen) marked "present" at Wingate or South Shore High School but were cutting their afternoon classes? Or were both the South Shore and Wingate students simply absent from school that day to play basketball? Hanging out in parks instead of going to school and class can be disastrous and even unnecessary since Wingate High School had reported no serious incidents *inside* the school this school year.

THEORETICAL BACKGROUND

Studies of truancy take several interesting tacks. First, researchers explore the levels and constancy of missing school, amassing data on both "total days" not present, and the number of absence "episodes" (i.e., the number of blocks of time absent without an acceptable excuse). Thus, five consecutive days away from school or class unexcused could be recorded as "five days absent," as a single "truant episode" of five days duration, or both.

Second, the dominant concept in the area of truancy for at-risk student behavior—like other problem behavior, or deviance—was and is a "deficit model" (Jessor & Jessor, 1977). Consequently, attributes of truants are examined and analyzed, seeking to find personal characteristics or student qualities that might correlate with serious non-attendance, including, students' sex (e.g., do boys cut more than girls?); socioeconomic status (do the poor miss more days than middle-class students?); ethnicity (Latinos more than Anglo-Whites?); and grade level (in high school, do younger students skip more than upper-class pupils?). Some scholars maintain that the "good students" miss fewer days while the "problem kids" are more often absent for unacceptable reasons.

Third, truancy is treated and measured as a handy proxy or indicator of more profound school problems and may thus be attacked in concert (through teamwork) with overall school planning and improvement. As Murgatroyd and Morgan (1992) explain in their book on Total Quality Management (TQM) in education, "If a school wants to tackle truancy, an effective team needs information about truancy within the school over time (preferably over many years) by age, by time of day, by gender, by ability, and by predictability. It may also need to examine the truants' own explanation for their behavior" (p. 157). Note the emphasis on the student and the source of the problem, not the school's culture and general student behaviors.

Finally, the causes of truancy have only recently been examined—with three theories of the root causes emerging: (1) a *character flaw* or *personal deficit*—a weakness in truants, even a kind of personal pathology, for deviants who cannot fit into the regime of the school and fail; (2) a destructive *culture* of truancy where some students negatively influence others, perhaps explaining why students often admit to "hanging out" with friends instead of attending school or class; and (3) a *rational choice* made by virtually all students during their educational careers: whether to attend or decline, based on balancing their self-interest and boredom; the real chances of getting caught and their parents/guardians being alerted; and the consequences of their actions for their future grades and post-high school plans.

Each theory rests on very different logic, theories, and perspectives. Truancy can be seen, then, as a personal student failing or problem—mainly a psychological viewpoint; a cultural norm common among rebellious teenagers—a sociological view; or a contextual response among virtually all students to the "working conditions" of their schools—an econo-political rationale.

Truancy: A Personal Deficit or Problem

One school of thought on truancy "blames" the character and upbringing of students who actively sabotage their own learning, grades, and futures. This explanation rests on a highly individualized viewpoint, one focusing on the traits of students who are "lazy," "slackers," and "goof-offs," and who must be pursued and brought back to school. The so-called truant officer—now called an attendance director—is pictured visiting homes in poverty and neglect, chasing erstwhile students from the street to the pool hall, and prevailing upon them not to give up on themselves, the school, and what education can do for them in life. Legal actions, too, can be taken against parents for "contributing to the delinquency of minors" and students for shirking their legally circumscribed responsibilities.

According to this model, adolescents behave recklessly because of a combination of deficits, disorders, or difficulties with learning. Also, family problems are considered significant contributors to students' shortcomings. Truancy is one of those means of "acting out" that social scientists have attempted to explain using the deficit model. Related to their deficit, some social scientists argue, is the nature of truancy (and other "acting out" behaviors). It is fun.

In social science language, fun has been conceptualized and operationalized as "sensation seeking" (Zuckerman, 1984). Sensation seeking is the degree to which a person seeks novelty and the intensity of experience. Truancy, the thrill of "getting away with it," and the freedom and range of activities following cutting school qualify as a means of sensation seeking.

Leithwood and Aiken (1995), however, see a much longer process whereby students lose faith in their school, become alienated, quit attending, and eventually drop out:

> For many students, dropping out of school is the final step in *a long process of gradual disengagement and reduced participation* in the formal curriculum of the school, as well as in the school's co-curriculum and more informal school life. Variation in schools' retention rates are likely to be predicted well from estimates of student participation [or truancy] and identification. (1995, p. 57)

Jeremy Finn (1989) similarly points to students' attendance, involvement, and success as closely related to a sense of "belongingness" or "engagement" combined with participation (p. 123).

A Culture of Truancy

Other theories of truant behavior in education attribute greater weight to the influence of the peer group in student life and decision making. How can a student stand up to peer pressure to "play hooky," these researcher query, when adolescents and pre-adolescents crave acceptance and the chance to prove their mettle with friends? In one study, 84 percent of all truants said that their friends had also skipped school; and 71 percent furthermore said their friends were involved in delinquent behavior (Levine, 1984).

Thus, schools confront more than the lone, troubled, deficient, misbehaving youth. Educators must deal with the "kid culture" of rebellion, a need for acceptance, and an easy, attractive avenue of misbehavior: let us cut class or school and see the world outside. This sociological perspective attempts to relate truancy to group norms, pressures, and the sanctioning of action. The concept of the "street corner society"—so popular in the 1950s and 1960s—is still very much a part of analysis and explanations of truancy in the literature.

A Rational Choice Theory of Truancy

A third explanation of truancy among students treats the behavior within an institutional context—where participants respond to the demands (rules) and expectations (norms) using a mental calculus. As "rational consumers" of education, virtually all students—not just the deviants or groups of troublemakers—make careful determinations about which classes to attend or skip, based on some or all of these factors: (a) the importance of the day's lesson or course of study to their grades and standing; (b) their excitement or boredom with the curriculum and pedagogy; (c) their chances of getting caught for going truant; (d) their likelihood that if caught, parents/guardians will be notified and called to school; and (e) the punishment, if any, that might be meted out by school officials.

Some evidence exists, then, that students make fairly sophisticated calculations and decisions, weighing the pros and cons of attending school or class, taking risks based on the costs of cutting against the benefits of attending, and thus "test the system" to see how far they can go. Perhaps, stricter teachers, teachers with exciting classrooms and demanding curricula, and schools with stated rules of attendance and firm enforcement are less likely to have high rates of truancy—while schools with "soft" or no rules and sloppy consequences for truancy may encourage students to stay away from school or classes. In this context, truancy is neither purely a teenage psycho-pathology nor a mode of cultural bonding and acceptance, but rather a more rational process of decision making as students learn to "read" their situations and act accordingly.

Theories of rational choice-making and "purposive action" (Coleman, 1990) explains how students might be exercising their power to choose, even though this right is officially denied them under school-attendance laws. Coleman, a leading theorist of the "rights to act," in his magnum opus, *Foundations of Social Theory* (1990), writes: "The essential quality of a right lies in its social base. Rights come into existence, vanish, and are taken from one actor and given to another by social recognition" (p. 63). True, but what of "rights to act" that are not sanctioned by legal authority? Coleman continues: "Yet rights are dependent on *power for their enforcement*, either the power of the holder of the right to protect his claim or the power of actors other than the holder to enforce their allocation of rights" (1990, p. 63). This power clearly resides with the state, the government, and local authorities.

What makes truancy a particularly interesting case of rational choice-making is that students and their culture actually sanction cutting based on their own calculations, while the adults either deny these choices to youth or tacitly approve of missing school by not moving aggressively against it. Perhaps, in the trade-off between trying to enforce school attendance and just letting young people "do their thing," students hold the upper hand: they outnumber adults by sixteen to one in schools in the United States; and playing hooky is believed to be such a minor offense (adults "take days off" too) that the authorities turn their heads and quietly support the students' choice.

Some teachers may actually welcome the truancy of certain students: those who are disruptive, threatening or just unwilling to cooperate. We've heard teachers say: "We got so much done today in math because Tommy Butler was absent and Sally Randolf didn't show up second period." Truancy is an unoffical way in some schools to lower class size and provide greater attention to those students in class. This message that a particular student is unwelcome in class probably comes through to students—and they make an informed choice to stay away.

Coleman explains the partial imposition of adult norms on younger people in his theory of "structures of action." He states:

Acceptance of the legitimacy of others' rights to partially control his or her action is necessary to establish the norm that gives him or her a legitimate right to control others' similar actions. Rejection of that legitimacy constitutes a rejection of the norm, an action against the legitimacy of his right on those other occasions. (1990, p. 288)

Hence, as students test and reject the norm that they must attend school daily, they may also be rejecting the legitimacy of other school norms and practices.

Thus, in summary, one school of thought "blames" the weakness of students who sabotage their own learning opportunities, while another viewpoint sees truancy as a reasoned response to a system of opportunity and control wherein students as consumers/conscripts play the system and decide if they can cut with impunity—academically, socially, and behaviorally. Students may also look to friends, depending on their "group think" about the situation and go along with the crowd (herd).

Other "Good" Reasons

And not a few students may stay home from school for personally legitimate—if officially unsanctioned—reasons, such as having to tend a sick sibling or parent (or grandparent), or assume other household responsibilities (e.g., taking a loved one to the doctor, going to the electric company to pay a monthly bill, or applying for an after-school job). Then, too, some students may simply oversleep, awakening in the morning to an empty house (with parents/guardians leaving for their work early), and go back to sleep, missing the first one or two classes in the morning. By 10:00 AM, it may be less embarrassing to stay home rather than trying to explain tardiness to school authorities.

Truancy, like other negative school behaviors, may become a self-reinforcing downward spiral—the more time missed from lessons, the further behind a student becomes—the less the incentive to attend—the higher the level of truancy and the poorer the performance. Failure to attend class breeds failure to achieve, which breeds a disincentive to continue the educational process.

And everyone loses: schools have lower morale and often forfeit state funds based on average daily attendance; teachers confront a revolving door of students in class; and students miss connecting with the class and school's program. Whatever the causes, much can be learned by asking students themselves about truancy. The methods and results are discussed in the next chapter.

2

Truancy Analyzed: The Students' View

Despite all the research and the competing theories of why students are truant, less is known from students themselves about their own reasons for attending or skipping. An earlier survey by Stoll and O'Keeffe (1989), administered to 789 pupils in nine government (public) schools in England, was an important beginning, and forms the starting point for this study of truancy among young people in the United States. This United States study explores the nature of truancy—both illegally missing school altogether (what Stoll and O'Keeffe call "blanket truancy") and cutting class ("post-registration truancy"), where a student is officially present in school but decides to be absent from certain or all classes.

The current study is based on a survey of a random group of some 230 public students in five schools in the United States of America and explores the following four assumptions.

1. To what extent are both kinds of truancy (cutting class and school) widespread among youth of all types, or is truancy the particular behavior of groups differentiated by race, sex, school, or academic standing?

   The study seeks, first of all, to determine to what degree truancy is associated with student characteristics (sex, age, race, academic standing) and feelings about their schools. Thus, this line of research seeks to test the degree to which truancy is related to a personal characteristic or if it is more a decision made by virtually all students regardless of their background.

2. To what degree does the likelihood of getting caught, having parents informed, and receiving punishment (e.g., detention or revocation of privileges) enter into students' determination of whether to be absent from school and/or class?

The study analyzes the students' personal perceptions of the context in which truancy appears. These include the incidence of "getting caught" being truant, the times that the home was alerted and the punishments applied. Again, we seek to understand to what degree students calculate their absences in a rational fashion: based on the context in which cutting and skipping are to occur.

3. To what degree do positive school, home, and personal characteristics correlate with better school and class attendance patterns?

Using six sub-scales from the survey instrument STAR-II or the *Student Truancy and Attendance Review* (see Appendix), we seek to understand more about the feelings of students toward their schools, themselves, their teachers, their parents, and the structure and rules concerning truancy, as possible determinants of cutting. Thus, if students are doing poorly in school academically and/or have uncaring teachers and parents, few supportive peers, an unattractive, poorly run school, low personal self-esteem, and fuzzy if any school rules defining and controlling school attendance, then are they also more likely to be truant than students with positive supports in these areas?

4. What collective action might be taken at school and home to enhance the educational offerings while making clear the rules and consequences of cutting and skipping?

Finally, we apply knowledge about students' experiences and feelings around truancy to practical ideas for taking action: for example, the possibility of making schools and homes happier and more supportive, while having the "rules of the game" made much clearer and more consistent. What might be done in light of these findings to dispel some of the myths about truancy (e.g., that it's the "bad" kids who are truant and skipping school while the "goody-goodies" always attend)? How might school leaders, working with students, attack the truancy problems at their roots: in the perceptions and calculations of students about their own education. From this "student's-eye" view of truancy, certain new realities may emerge. These insights can be translated into policies and programs to reduce truancy by engaging the school, home, and community in the process.

STUDENT SURVEY SAMPLE

These data were gathered from some 230 high school and middle school students (ages thirteen through twenty-one), using the *Student Truancy and Attendance Review* (STAR—II) instrument, in part developed in England and modified in the United States of America. As shown in Tables 2.1 and 2.2, the composition of the sample included students from a variety of *ethnic and racial backgrounds* (African American, Latino/Latina, Anglo-White, Asian, and "Other"), from grades eighth through twelfth, by sex, by academic attainment (Excellent = A/B+, Good = B/B−, Fair = C/C−/D), and Failing = F), and by age. Among the groups, the Asian American students tended to be too few in this sample, making real analysis of their attitudes and behaviors difficult.

Table 2.1 shows the characteristics of the students in the sample. The sex breakdown was 55.5 percent or 127 male students and 102 or 44.5 percent female (see part a). Among the five school grade levels, 17.9 percent were eighth graders; 19.7 percent in ninth; 35.8 percent tenth graders, the largest cohort; 9.2 percent eleventh graders; and 17.4 percent twelfth graders.

Thus, only the eleventh grade seemed undersubscribed. See Table 2.1, part b. Ethnic/racial breakdown was interesting in these high schools, with a majority being nonwhite: African Americans numbered seventy-three or 34.6 percent; Latino/Latina, fifty-four pupils or 25.6 percent; Anglo-Whites, thirty or 14.2 percent; Asian Americans (the smallest group) included only five students or 2.4 percent; and "Other" forty-nine or 23.2 percent, for a total of 211 of the 230 students giving their ethnicity and the remainder leaving the ethnicity item blank. Finally, when asked how much English was spoken in the home, versus other languages, 161 or 70.9 percent said "Yes," English was the home language, while 19.8 percent said that English was spoken "Sometimes," and 9.3 percent or twenty-one students indicated, "No, English." Hence, 29.1 percent of the sample students checked that non-English was spoken in the home either all or some of the time.

Table 2.1.   Characteristics of Sample Students

Quality:		*Frequency*	*% of Total*
a. Sex			
	Male	127	55.5
	Female	102	44.5
	Total	229	100.0
b. Grade Level	8th Grade	41	17.9
	9th Grade	45	19.7
	10th Grade	82	35.8
	11th Grade	21	9.2
	12th Grade	40	17.4
	Total	229	100.0
c. Ethnicity:	African American	73	34.6
	Latino/Latina	54	25.6
	Anglo-White	30	14.2
	Asian	5	2.4
	"Other"	49	23.2
	Total	211	100.0
d. English Spoken at Home?			
	Yes	161	70.9
	Sometimes	45	19.8
	No	21	9.3
	Total	227	100.0

Table 2.2 shows the *age distribution* of the students, with the average of the survey participants being 15.62 years old (s.d. = 1.53; N = 206) with a range of eight years between the youngest sample pupils at thirteen and the oldest at twenty-one years of age. Frequencies of sample student ages were the following: the thirteen-year-old category included eighteen students or 8.7 percent of the sample (who filled in the item); age fourteen numbered thirty-one students or 15.0 percent; age fifteen was the largest at 25.2 percent with sixteen-year-olds next with forty-six students (22.3 percent); seventeen-year-olds included thirty-six pupils or 17.5 percent; eighteen-year-olds, seventeen or 8.3 percent; nineteen-year-olds 2.4 percent or five students, with no twenty-year-olds and one twenty-one-year-old (0.4%).

When asked about work after school—a pressure that might tire students if they also had to do their homework after work—the sample showed that 31.7 percent or seventy-two students had some kind of job:

Table 2.2.   Age Distribution and After-School Work of Sample Students

		Frequency	Percentage
e. Age Distribution	13 yrs. old	18	8.7
	14 yrs. old	31	15.0
	15 yrs. old	52	25.2
	16 yrs. old	46	22.3
	17 yrs. old	36	17.5
	18 yrs. old	17	8.3
	19 yrs. old	5	2.4
	21 yrs. old	1	0.4
	Total	206	100.0
f. Work After School			
	Yes—Regularly	49	21.6
	Yes—Sometimes	23	10.2
	No, None	155	68.2
	Total:	227	100.0

21.6 percent having "regular work," and 10.2 percent, "sometimes" work, leaving 155 or 68.2 percent with no after-school jobs reported. (See Table 2.2.)

Sample students attended five different schools, four high schools and a middle school. Table 2.3 shows the sample size from each school, the number of male and female students, their ages, grades, and school size. Except for School B, we see a balance by sex. Overall, we have a reasonable balance across the schools by these qualities.

Table 2.3.   Sample School Characteristics

	School A	School B	School C	School D	School E	Total
1. Sample Size	51	47	40	43	49	230
2. School Type	High School	High School	High School	Middle School	High School	High School
3. By Gender	Boys: 24 Girls: 26	Boys: 36 Girls: 11	Boys: 21 Girls: 19	Boys: 21 Girls: 22	Boys: 25 Girls: 24	Boys: 127 Girls: 103
4. By Grade Level	8th = 1 9th = 28 10th = 19 11th = 2 12th = 1	8th = 0 9th = 15 10th = 16 11th = 12 12th = 4	8th = 0 9th = 0 10th = 0 11th = 5 12th = 35	8th = 40 9th = 2 10th = 0 11th = 0 12th = 0	8th = 0 9th = 0 10th = 47 11th = 2 12th = 0	8th = 41 9th = 45 10th = 82 11th = 21 12th = 40

LEVELS OF TRUANCY

A major purpose of this research is to analyze the truancy process as we conceived it in the following seven related actions:

1. *Measures of Cutting:* The truancy cycle begins with an analysis of two types of truancy: missing school altogether and missing classes (but being marked "in attendance" at school).
2. *Cutting to Where?* Students may come to school and then miss classes by leaving the school building or not. This measure only applies to truancy occurring after students are considered at school (registered).
3. *Measures of Students' Being Truant by Pretending to Be Sick or in Need of Help:* Sometimes students make up excuses to get out of attending a class: being ill and requesting to see the school nurse; needing to check on lost items; needing to see a teacher or counselor; needing to call home or using a fake doctor's note. This measure only pertains to students who attend school but find excuses for getting out of classes, not students who never came to school that day.
4. *Measures of Cutting "With Whom"?*: Students may miss school or just class with friends or do it alone. If we are to understand the causes of truancy among students, we need some information on the sociology of the action, including measures of whether students are truant in groups or solo.
5. *Measures of Getting Caught:* Students may or may not be caught in the act of truancy by school authorities. Measuring the frequency of getting caught gives a sense of the consequences for students of their actions.
6. *Measures of Being Reported to Parents/Guardians:* School authorities may decide to call the parents, both to alert them of the absences of their children but also to bring leverage from home to help to stop the cutting. This measure, again, gives some sense of the school's reaction to truancy and their level of aggressive action to prevent or reduce the problem.
7. *Measures of Being Punished for Truancy:* Finally, in the truancy process, students may receive official reprimands and other bad conduct actions. On the STAR-II (*Student Truancy and Attendance Review*) instrument, we asked students how often they were punished and how.

Order of Questions	"Blanket" Truancy Skipping School	"Post-Roll Call" Truancy Cutting Class
1. Cutting Behavior?	—	—
2. Leaving the Building?	(Already truant)	—
3. Cutting With Friends?	—	—
4. Pretending to Need Help? A Ploy to Cut	(No—not at school)	—
5. Getting Caught?	—	—
6. Being Reported to Home?	—	—
7. Being Punished for Truancy?	—	—

Figure 2.1. Structure of this Study, as Applied to School (Blanket) and Classroom (Post-Registration)Truancy

Figure 2.1 shows the two types of truancy and the seven different areas studied in this research. Note that five out of the seven variables related behaviors that apply to both types of truancy since students who are not at school can neither "go off campus" with friends nor seek a diversionary tactic (pretending) at school to get out of class. A menstrual period, a sharp pain, a headache, and the need to call home will all do. The data are now presented in roughly these seven steps.

THE RESULTS

First, we ascertained the levels of truancy from both school ("blanket" truancy) and classroom ("post-registration" truancy) and second, we then analyzed the particular characteristics of these cutters and skippers versus those attending. And as we shall show, truancy was more common across all groups (male/female, older and younger, ethnic groups, etc.) than the literature would have indicated. And, the United States data were quite similar to the larger study done by Stoll and O'Keeffe in England in 1989.

• *Cutting Class or Skipping School:* The first finding was that truancy was much more widespread than anticipated, particularly "class cutting," which appears more popular than skipping school altogether. As shown in table 2.4, of the students surveyed, 67.8 percent—or 154 out of 227 answering the question—admitted to being absent from certain *classes*, with 54.6 percent indicating "Sometimes" and 13.1 percent "Often." This contrasts with the 38.1 percent (or 86 students out of 221) who skipped school completely, with 29.9 percent missing school "Sometimes" and 9.1 percent "Often."

Table 2.4. Comparison of Truancy: School v. Class

	Frequency	Percent
"Never" Cut Class (N = 227)	73	32.1
"Never" Cut School (N = 221)	135	61.1
"Sometimes" Cut Class	124	54.6
"Sometimes" Cut School	66	29.9
"Often" Cut Class	30	13.1
"Often" Cut School	20	9.1
Total Cutting—		
(N = 227) by Class	154	67.8
(N = 221) by School	86	38.1

• *Truancy by Sample School Sites:* Table 2.5 presents information on school truancy by the five separate school sites represented in this sample. While the average for cutting at all schools is 38.9 percent, the range among the schools on this type of truancy runs from a low at School D at 24.4 percent (see column 4, row 3) to the highest blanket truancy at School C with 52.3 percent being truant in some way. When the degree of cutting school is analyzed as cutting "Sometimes," Schools B, D, and E are the highest at 81.0 percent for School B, 80 percent for D, and 100 percent recorded "Sometimes" at School E.

Table 2.5. School Truancy by Building Site

Truancy by School	School A	School B	School C	School D	School E	All School Total
Cut School Sometimes	13 (61.9%)	17 (81.0%)	15 (71.4%)	8 (80.0%)	13 (100%)	66 (76.7%)
Cut School Often	8 (38.1%)	4 (19.1%)	6 (28.6%)	2 (20.0%)	0 (0%)	20 (23.3%)
Total Cuts	21 (43.8%)	21 (47.7%)	21 (52.5%)	10 (24.4%)	17 (34.7%)	86 (38.9%)
Never Cut School	26 (54.2%)	23 (52.3%)	19 (47.5%)	31 (75.6%)	36 (73.5%)	135 (61.1%)
Total Sample	48 (100%)	44 (100%)	40 (100%)	41 (100%)	49 (100%)	221 (100%)

Here is a listing of the "outliers" in cutting school with Total, Often, and Sometimes Cut:
Outlier Schools for Truancy (Blanket): Total Cuts: High = School C (52.5%) Low = School D (24.4%) Average = All Schools (38.9%)
"Often" Cuts: High = School A (38.1%) Low = School B (19.1%) Average = All Schools (23.3%)
"Sometimes" Cuts: High = School D (80%) Low = School A (61.9%) Average = All Schools (76.7%)

And "Often" goes from 0 percent at School E, to 38.1 percent at School A. Among the "Never Cut" schools, two were in the low 50 percent (School A at 54.4 percent and School B at 52.3 percent), two at the low 70 percent (School D at 75.6 percent and School E at 73.5 percent), and one in the middle (School C at 47.5 percent). Thus the range is nearly 23 percentage points between the high outlier and the low. We found no significant difference in truancy levels among the five sites, as indicated by the Chi Square (2.26, d.f. = 3) of expected variance: p = .521.

Table 2.6 presents data by school location on *classroom* truancy: that is, students who are "at school" but who cut classes during the regular school day. When these data are analyzed for each of the five sample schoolbuildings, we see a far higher level of cutting and more divergence among sample locations. Total classroom cutting ran just over two-thirds of all students (67.8 percent, as shown in column 6, line 3) regardless of school location. However, when we look at the "high" and "low" schools on overall class-cutting, School C had 90.0 percent missing some days, with the low at School D with 41.9 percent. Schools B and E were close together in school truancy at 66.7 percent at School B and 65.3 percent at School E.

When the level of school truancy is examined, we see over a quarter of the students (26.3 percent) at School A and 22.2 percent at School C cutting school "Often," with the lows at School B (6.7 percent) and School D at 5.6 percent. Cutting "Sometimes" shows a different rank order, with Schools B and D at over 90 percent (School B = 93.3 percent and School D = 94.3

Table 2.6. Cutting Class by Building Site

Truancy by School	School A	School B	School C	School D	School E	All School Total
Cut School Often	10 (26.3%)	2 (6.7%)	8 (22.2%)	1 (5.6%)	9 (28.1%)	30 (19.5%)
Cut School Sometimes	28 (73.7%)	28 (93.3%)	28 (77.8%)	17 (94.4%)	23 (71.9%)	124 (80.5%)
Total Cuts % of Total Sample	38 (76.0%)	30 (66.7%)	36 (90.0%)	18 (41.9%)	32 (65.3%)	154 (67.8%)
Never Cut School	12 (24.0%)	15 (33.3%)	4 (10.0%)	25 (58.1%)	17 (34.7%)	73 (32.2%)
Total Sample	50 (100%)	45 (100%)	40 (100%)	43 (100%)	49 (100%)	227 (100%)

percent); the lower ranking "Sometimes" cutting classes schools were School E at 71.9 percent and School A at 73.7 percent, with the overall all-school average running about 81 percent. We found high levels of significance with a Chi Square of 31.43 (d.f. = 8, p = .0001).

In sum, the contrast between being truant from school or individual classes gives some weight to the notion that students are more clinical, almost surgical in their cutting: they apparently come to school and then "blow off" certain classes that they find unimportant, troublesome, or easily cut. Thus, while the commonly held belief is that truancy is the behavior of troublesome students suffering some deficit or another, these data indicate that over two-thirds of students in this sample tried unexcused absences on occasion or regularly. At a few schools, the cutting class level was 90 percent and 76 percent, with a low at 42 percent, showing the range of the problem.

These U.S. findings compare closely (67.8 percent in the United States to 66.1 percent in England) with the data gathered in England by Stoll and O'Keeffe (1989). These authors explain

> that 765 pupils completed the questionnaire and of those boys and girls, 506 (66.1 percent) admitted being truant. This was a surprisingly high number of pupils, especially since the schools which took part in this survey are considered to be "good" schools, popular with parents and, in several cases, oversubscribed. (Stoll & O'Keeffe, 1989, pp. 51–52)

CHARACTERISTICS OF TRUANTS AND SCHOOL ACTIONS

Further analysis is necessary to relate the characteristics of truants and the school's responses to truancy by students' sex (gender), age, grade level, academic performance, and other qualities. We also investigate the important relationship between students' feelings and perceptions of their environment (teachers, parents, school administration, extra-curriculum, academic progress, and selves) and their truancy.

1. Truancy by Sex Differences

Here again, we confront a myth about truancy: that somehow the "bad boys" cut class and school while the "good girls" do not; that female students act differently, and that school authorities handle truancy differently by the gender of the students. This myth, as we shall show, fits nicely into the "blaming the student" approach, based on gender-related deficit theories of personality development and adolescent (mis)behavior.

As *Time* magazine described, two policemen in the Bronx (New York City) had created "a 1950s-style anti-truancy program," launched by a new, 1950s-style mayor Rudolf Giuliani of New York City" (Rubin, 1994, p. 22). The police officers' efforts to catch and return truants to school were indicative of the problems and the differing behaviors of girls and boys. The article explains:

> Cruising along East 182nd Street, the officers describe the finer points of pursuit. Traditionally, says Officer DiAngelo, truants were predominately boys, "but girls are cutting more now." Girls, Officer Krajecksi says, "are always 'sick' or 'late.' They don't run as much [as boys]. Solos never run; groups [of students] usually do." (Rubin, 1994, p. 22).

Truancy by Student Gender

As shown in table 2.7, when the data are compared by sex, we see that the sexes are truant from *class* at about the same rate. Since the data set had 124 male students and only 102 female respondents, we needed a means of standardizing by sample size. Consequently, we used the percent

Table 2.7. Cutting Class: Comparing Male and Female Student Behavior

	Male	*Female*	*Both*
1. Cut Class Often	19	11	30
	(22.9%)	(15.7%)	(19.6%)
2. Cut Class Sometimes	64	59	123
	(77.1%)	(84.3%)	(80.4%)
	(100.0%)	(100.0%)	(100.0%)
3. Total Cutters Percent of Total. Line 5 below:	83 (66.9%)	70 (68.6%)	153 (67.7%)
4. Cut Class Never	41	32	73
	(33.1%)	(31.4%)	(32.3%)
5. Total by Group	(n=124)	(n=102)	(n=226)
	(100.0%)	(100.0%)	(100.0%)

within each sex category to eliminate the effects of a larger male sample. For example, of the 83 male students admitting to cutting class, 22.9 percent (19 pupils) did it "Often" and 77.1 percent or 64 pupils played hooky "Sometimes."

In comparison, of the 70 female pupils who cut class, 11 reported "Often" at 15.7 percent of total female cutters but a higher percent (84.3 percent) or 59 students out of 70 were missing class "Sometimes." Hence, when the 83 total male "cutters" out of 124 total males are compared to the 59 total female truants out of the total of 102 in the sample, we see that 66.9 percent were male and 68.6 percent were female—again coming very close to the combined truancy rate found in England. And when both sexes are combined, the 153 "post-registration" truants are 67.7 percent of the total sample answering these questions at 226 students.

Thus, comparisons within gender categories help to dispel the commonly-held belief that boys are the acting-outers and the students who break the rules, while girls are more conforming and well behaved. In fact, when a Chi-Square (1.31706, d.f. = 2, p = .5176) and Pearson's R on effect size ($-.02187, p = .3719$) were run on the data to test for significance by sex of students, we found no statistically significant difference between the male and female students' behaviors.

This finding lends some credibility to the thesis that female and male students—not based on their sex-related personality stereotypes—are just about as likely to "test the system" and make rational choices about which classes to attend or not. Hence, a typical predictor of human behavior, *sex*—as an explanatory variable for truancy—is called into question by this research.

Analysis of cutting school altogether by gender turns up some interesting findings. As table 2.8 shows, total school cutting is slightly higher for female students than male students at 36.9 percent for boys and 40.8 percent for girls. Even staying home "Often" is somewhat higher at 27.5 percent for girls compared to boys at 20.0 percent. Only at the cutting "Sometimes," as a percentage of total school truancy, do boys outscore girls at 80.0 percent compared to 72.5 percent for the female students. Both groups "Never" cut school at somewhat similar rates: 63.1 percent of males and 59.2 percent of the females. Overall, nearly 61.4 percent of this sample claimed "Never" to cut school.

Table 2.8.   School Truancy by Gender

	Male	Female	Both
Often Cut School	9 (20.0%)	11 (27.5%)	20 (23.5%)
Sometimes Cut	36 (80.0%)	29 (72.5%)	65 (76.5%)
Total Cuts of School	45 (36.9%)	40 (40.8%)	85 (38.6%)
Never Cut School	77 (63.1%)	58 (59.2%)	135 (61.4%)
Total Sample	122 (100%)	98 (100%)	22 (100%)

Cutting Class To Where?

A second question relating the sex variable to school reactions to truant boys and girls is also informative. We asked students: If you were truant by skipping particular classes, did you "hide" in the building or did you leave the premises?

As shown in table 2.9, boys were slightly more likely to cut and leave the premises than girls: data on boys indicated that 39.6 percent stayed "Sometimes," 30.8 percent "Always" stayed, and 29.7 percent responded that they "Cut and Left the Building." Female respondents, meanwhile, were slightly higher with 45.1 percent "Staying Sometimes," with 28.2 percent "Cutting Class but Staying in the School Always," and 26.8 percent "Cut and Left." Thus, a slight difference between the sexes on location of cutting class was that nearly 30 percent of the boys who were truant left the building, compared to about 27 percent of the girls.

When both girls and boys are considered together, we see that 42.0 percent stayed in the school building "Sometimes," 29.6 percent "Always Stayed," and 28.4 percent "Cut and Left." Thus, the pattern does not indicate that the innocent girls dutifully went to class while the mischievous boys were "hanging out" in their schools. In fact, girls were more likely to cut and leave "Sometimes" while boys were slightly more likely to "Cut and Leave" (girls = 26.8 percent versus boys = 29.7 percent). Among the "Did Not Cut," male students showed 24.8 percent (30 out of 121) in comparison to 29 percent (29 of 100) for female students. The total rate of "Not" cutting for both gender groups together was 26.7 percent (59 of 221 students).

Table 2.9.   Cutting Behavior of Male and Female Pupils: Cutting To Where?
"Did You Cut Class and Leave the School?"

Cutting Groups	Male	Female	Both
Sometimes Stayed in the Building	36	32	68
(% of Cutters)	(39.6%)	(45.1%)	(42.0%)
Always Stayed in the Building	28	20	48
(% of Cutters)	(30.8%)	(28.2%)	(29.6%)
Cut and Left the Building	27	19	46
(% of Cutters)	(29.7%)	(26.8%)	(28.4%)
Total Cutters	91	71	162
	(75.2%)	(71.0%)	(73.3%)
Did *Not* Cut Class at All	30	29	59
(% of Total)	(24.8%)	(29.0%)	(26.7%)
Total Sample Pupils and %	121	100	221
	(100%)	(100%)	(100%)

Again, we do not see the predicted pattern of boys' cutting and leaving the school in significantly higher numbers than girls; the Chi Square statistic (.99035, d.f. = 3) was not Significant (.8036), nor did the Pearson's R (.01202, p = .4395) show a significant relationship between gender and leaving the building during school hours.

Cutting With Whom?

Next, we inquired whether girls tend more than boys to cut school in groups ("With Friends") or alone: thus, to what degree is cutting a collective or individual act? Table 2.10 shows that girls are more "social" in their *class-cutting* activities, with 75 percent of the truant female students

Table 2.10.   Cutting Class: Alone or "With Friends" by Gender

	Male	Female	Both
"I Cut Alone"	29	18	47
	(32.5%)	(25.0%)	(29.2%)
"I Cut With Friends"	60	54	114
	(67.4%)	(75%)	(70.8%)
Total Cutters	89	72	161
	(100.%)	(100%)	(100%)

doing it with friends (54 out of 72 students who cut), compared to 67.4 percent among the boys. When combined by sex, the total of 70.8 percent cut with friends, meaning that peer support for both sexes is important to the truancy process.

Hence, the data show that girls do cut and do it with others, giving credence to both the student "culture" theory of truancy and the rational approach since girls do it too. Tests of gender differences show a Chi Square of 1.13734, d.f. = 2, and Significance at .2341 and a Pearson's R of .04872, p = .2341—indicating no significant difference between boys and girls in their truancy behaviors, nor a significant relationship between gender and with whom students cut.

Data on being truant from *school* (blanket truancy) with friends or alone by the sex of the student show somewhat different results than cutting classes with or without company. As presented in table 2.11, the boys tend to non-attend school with cronies at 72.4 percent of the time, compared to the female students at 69 percent, although the data do show high levels of joint cutting of school: averaging for both sexes at 71 percent. The differences between the sexes on cutting with a friend or alone show no significance using the Chi Square statistic, (1.68475, d.f. = 3; p = .6403); and the Pearson's R = .05440, p = .2128).

Getting Caught Cutting Class by Sex of Student

Since we know that male and female students are truant at about the same rate, at least in this sample, the next question is: Are students caught as truants from class at about the same rate—male and female—as they

Table 2.11. Cutting School with Whom? By Gender (Blanket Truancy)

With Whom	Male	Female	Both
1. Skipping School Alone	16 (27.6%)	13 (31.0%)	29 (29.0%)
2. Skipping School with Friends	42 (72.4%)	29 (69.0%)	71 (71.0%)
3. Total School Skippers	58 (49.2%)	42 (43.3%)	100 (46.5%
4. Not Being Truant	60 (50.8%)	55 56.7%)	115 (53.5%)
5. Total Sample	118 (100%)	97 (100%)	215 (100%)

are cutting? As shown in table 2.12, the data indicate some interesting similarities and differences. Boys got "Caught Once" for being truant from *class* at a higher rate (29.1 percent) than girls (23.5 percent); however, getting caught "More than Once" appears to be almost equally divided between the sexes (boys = 22.8 percent/girls = 22.1 percent), while cutting and "Never" getting caught favors females at 54.4 percent compared to males at 48.1 percent. Thus, getting caught "Once" is more common among boys; similarly, girls "Never" get caught more often than boys, by about 6 percent. When we tested for significance in differences by student sex, we found none: Chi Square = 1.59392, d.f., = 3, and = .6653; and a weak, not significant correlation with a Pearson's R = 14.550, p = .1091.

Overall, students of both sexes taken together got caught once at a rate of 26.5 percent, more than once 22.5 percent of the time, and just over half (51 percent) never get caught, meaning that in this sample around 49.0 percent get caught for being truant, higher than previously noted. Thus, over a four-year high school career, about half of the students (who are truant) are likely to get snagged by the authorities for not attending classes. See table 2.12, column 3.

Similar analysis on students cutting *school* (blanket truancy) saw somewhat different results. No female students admitted to having been caught several times, although 30 percent or 12 were actually apprehended once. However, 70.0 percent of the girls who cut school indicated that they had never been caught, while only 54.7 percent of the boys had escaped undetected.

The combined gender data on *school* truancy are somewhat different from the cutting *class* findings: that is, the rate of truancy of this type ("blanket truancy") is lower at 43.7 percent or 93 students in this total

Table 2.12.   Rates of Getting Caught Cutting Class by Gender

Getting Caught	Male	Female	Both
1. Caught Once	23 (29.1%)	16 (23.5%)	39 (26.5%)
2. Caught More than Once	18 (22.8%)	15 (22.1%)	33 (22.5%)
3. Cut Class—But Never Caught	38 (48.1%)	37 (54.4%)	75 (51.0%)
4. Total	79 (100%)	68 (100%)	147 (100%)

Table 2.13. Rates of Getting Caught Cutting School by Gender

Getting Caught	Male	Female	Both
1. Caught Once	9	0	9
	(17.0%)	(0%)	(9.7%)
2. Caught More than Once	15	12	27
	(28.3%)	(30.0%)	(29.0%)
3. Cut Class—but *Never* Caught	29	28	57
	(54.7%)	(70.0%)	(61.3%)
4. Total Cutting Students	53	40	93
% of Total	(44.5%)	(42.6%)	(43.7%)
5. No-Cutting Students	66	54	120
	(55.5%)	57.5%	(56.3%)
6. Total	119	94	213
	(100%)	(100%)	(100%)

group, compared to the *class* cutting rate for both boys and girls combined at 49.0 percent or 71 pupils. And among the boys, the school-skipping rate was 44.5 percent, compared to 42.6 percent for girls. These findings seem to indicate that girls are better at beating the system and its effort to catch these rule-breakers. Perhaps, schools give girls the benefit of the doubt when they are absent, accepting their excuses more readily than the boys'.

One must assume that both girls and boys are marked absent by schools consistently and equitably; it's in the processing of the reasons for these absences that girls may be better at "getting off" and their excuses may be accepted with more trust. Further analysis shows that the differences between the sexes were mildly significant, with the Chi Square of 7.7230 with d.f. = 3, and a significance level of .0532.

Notifying the Home of Truancy by Sex of Student

Another theme in this research is whether schools treat truants differently, based on such characteristics as sex (age, grade level, race/ethnicity, etc.). Table 2.14 presents the analysis by student gender of how often, when students are caught being absent from class but on the "present" roster that day, that the school notifies their parents or guardians.

Interestingly, the percentages are very close between the sexes, with 42.9 percent of the boys indicating that their home was notified of their cutting while 41.2 percent of the girls recording their home called. The overall rate

Table 2.14.   School Notifying Home for Students' Cutting Class by Gender

	Male	Female	Both
1. Notify Home of Cutting	36	28	64
	(49.2%)	(41.2%)	(42.1%)
2. Cut, but No Home Notified	48	40	88
	(57.1%)	(58.8%)	(57.9%)
3. Total Cutting	84	68	152
% of Total Students	(68.9%)	(68.0%)	(68.5%)
4. Non-Cutting Students	38	32	70
% of Total Pupils	(31.2%)	(32.0%)	(31.5%)
Total Sample	122	100	222
	(100%)	(100%)	(100%)

for both genders was 42.1 percent. The test of significance showed no significant difference between the sexes on calling home: the Chi Square = .87871, d.f. = 3, p = .8308; Pearson's R = −.01030, p = .4312.

Thus, the home is not told that their offspring (whether male or female) are cutting *class* about 58 percent of the time. Again, the sex of the student seems far less important than one might surmise in schools' acting decisively, if truancy were the activity of the "bad" kids and not a generalized phenomenon among all levels and both genders.

However, when considering students who are truant from *school* altogether, the data seem quite different. Table 2.15 shows that male students are nearly twice as likely to have their homes contacted than females: homes

Table 2.15.   School Notifying Home for Student "Blanket" Truancy (Skipping School) by Gender

	Male	Female	Both
1. Notify Home of Cutting	30	11	41
% of Cutting Students	(44.1%)	(23.4%)	(35.7%)
2. Cut, but *No* Home Notified	38	36	74
	(55.9%)	(76.6%)	(64.4%)
3. Total Cutting	68	47	115
% of Total Students	(58.1%)	(51.1%)	(55.0%)
4. Non-Cutting Students	49	45	94
% of Total Pupils	(35.9%)	(48.9%)	(45.5%)
Total Sample	117	92	209
	(100%)	(100%)	(100%)

of male students were contacted 44.1 percent compared to 23.4 percent for female students). Thus, of the 47 female "school cutters" in this sample, only 11 had their homes contacted. For both gender groups combined, notification of homes ran an average of 35.7 percent. That is, of the 115 truant students in this sample, 41 (35.7 percent) had their homes called, 74 (64.4 percent) students did not, and 94 (45.5 percent of total of 209) students indicated that they never were truant.

School Punishment for Being Truant by Gender

A last step in the process of preventing truancy is determining an appropriate "punishment" for not appearing and for thus for breaking the mandatory attendance laws. Comparing girls and boys should round out the picture of whether schools are confronting the problem and whether sex is a determinant of schools' reactions to students' being truant from both school and class (blanket and post-registration).

Table 2.16 shows the levels of punishment, if any, for missing school. Girls are more likely to get "Caught but Not punished," 79 percent for girls versus 71.2 percent for the boys, with an overall catch-and-let-go rate of 74.4 percent for both sexes together. Meanwhile, the boys who were caught were punished at a rate of 28.8 percent while the girls were dealt with at a 21.0 percent rate. Overall, only one-quarter of all students caught were reprimanded, or 25.6 percent (see column 3, row 2). Thus of the 43.3 percent of the students admitting in this question to cutting school, only

Table 2.16.   Being Punished for "Blanket" Truancy (Skipping School) by Gender

	Male	Female	Both
1. Caught but Not Punished	37	30	67
% of Cutting Students	(71.2%)	(79.0%)	(74.4%)
2. Caught and Punished	15	8	23
	(28.8%)	(21.0%)	(25.6%)
3. Total Cutting	52	38	90
% of Total Students	(45.6%)	(40.4%)	(43.3%)
4. Non-Cutting Students	62	56	118
% of Total Pupils	(54.4%)	(59.6%)	(56.7%)
5. Total Sample	114	94	208
	(100%)	(100%)	(100%)

25 or so percent were punished. The differences between boys and girls in being punished was not significant using the Chi Square (2.07779, d.f. = 3, .5563 and the Pearson's R = −.08205, p = .1188).

Analysis of punishment for cutting *class* appears a little different. As shown in table 2.17, girls were less likely to get punished if caught cutting class than boys, with 63.7 percent of the boys being caught and getting off, while 71.2 percent of the girls were released. Overall, these schools let go free 67.1 percent of the students caught for being truant from school. Hence, about one-third of the students who cut were punished, with 36.3 percent of the boys and 28.2 percent of the girls reporting that they were both caught and dealt with.

When asked exactly what their punishments were, most students left that item blank. However, some wrote that when they were caught cutting class, they were "punished for two weeks," "grounded," "sent to detention," "given de-merits," "given no privileges," and "whipped " (presumably at home). And for cutting school altogether, if caught, students listed that: "I was punished at home," "they beat me down," "I couldn't go outside for two weeks but I still watched TV," "I couldn't make phone calls," "No privileges, and most insightfully, " I was punished by my grade in classes"!

2. Truancy and Ethnic/Racial Differences

Truancy can also be analyzed by the ethnic and racial backgrounds of the students. This small sample of students, some 220, has a diverse mix of ethnic/racial and language groups—and we have data on the language

Table 2.17.   Being Punished for "Post-Registration" Truancy (Skipping Class) by Gender

	Male	Female	Both
1. Caught by Not Punished % of Cutting Students	51 (63.7%)	47 (71.2%)	98 (67.1%)
2. Caught and Punished	29 (36.3%)	19 (28.8%)	48 (32.9%)
3. Total Cutting % of Total Students	80 (69.0%)	66 (69.5%)	146 (69.2%)
4. Non-Cutting Students % of Total Pupils	36 (31.1%)	29 (30.5%)	65 (30.8%)
5. Total Sample	116 (100%)	95 (100%)	211 (100%)

spoken in the home to get a fix on the diversity of the sample respondents. The following discussion and presentations illustrate the relationship, if any, between ethnicity and truancy and its consequences.

Truancy by Ethnicity

When the school and classroom cutting data are segmented by racial/ethnic groups, as shown in tables 2.18, 2.19, and 2.20, the data show some interesting trends. Among the ethnic groups represented, as shown in table 2.18, the Latinos had the highest reported rate of "Never" cutting school with 69.2 percent; African Americans next at 66.7 percent; then "Other" (53.9 percent); and "Never Cut" is lowest overall among Anglo-White in this sample (51.6 percent), meaning that the White cutting school rate is highest. When we analyzed the category of students who do cut school, we see that African American students tend to cut "Often" at 44.4 percent, Whites next at 26.7 percent, and Latinos and Other are the lowest frequent school truants at 6.3 percent and 4.2 percent respectively. (The Asian rate is high at 60.0 percent but the sample is only 3.) When a test of significance was applied to ethnic differences for truancy from school, we found a significant difference with a Chi Square of 37.94, d.f. = 12, p = .0002.

An examination of the students across ethnic groups found truant from *classes* after arriving at school indicates that overall, 68.3 percent of all students cut classes. Of the cutters, 13.1 percent admitted skipping classes "Often" and 55.2 percent indicated "Sometimes." Of the total sample, 31.7 percent said "Never."

Table 2.18. School Truancy by Ethnic Group

	African American	Latino/ Latina	Anglo White	Asian American	Other	Total Groups
I Cut School Often	11 (44.0%)	1 (6.3%)	4 (26.7%)	3 (60.0%)	1 (4.2%)	20 (22.7%)
I Cut School Sometimes	14 (56.0%)	15 (93.7%)	11 (73.3%)	2 (40.0%)	23 (95.8%)	65 (76.5%)
Total School Cuts	25 (33.3%)	16 (30.8%)	15 (48.4%)	5 (100%)	24 (46.2%)	85 (39.5%)
Never Cut School	50 (66.7%)	36 (69.2%)	16 (51.6%)	0 (0%)	28 (53.9%)	130 (60.5%)
Total Sample	75 (100%)	52 (100%)	31 (100%)	5 (100%)	52 (100%)	225 (100%)

Table 2.19.   Truancy from Classes (Post Registration) by Ethnic Group

	African American	Latino/ Latina	Anglo White	Asian American	Other	Total Groups
1. Cut Often	10	5	5	3	6	29
% of Total	(12.8%)	(9.1%)	(16.1%)	(60.0%)	(11.5%)	(13.1%)
2. Cut Sometimes	40	28	22	2	30	122
	(51.3%)	(50.9%)	(71.0%)	(40.0%)	(57.7%)	(55.2%)
3. Cut Never	28	22	4	0	16	70
	(35.9%)	(40.0%)	(12.9%)	(0%)	(30.8%)	(31.7%)
4. Total Truants	50	33	27	5	36	151
	(64.1%)	(60.0%)	(87.1%)	(100%)	(69.2%)	(68.3%)
5. Total Sample	78	55	31	5	52	221
	(100%)	(100%)	(100%)	(100%)	(100%)	(100%)

By ethnic group, however, the Anglo-Whites had 16.1 percent of the cutters indicating skipping class "Often" and 71.0 percent "Sometimes," for a total of 87.1 percent cutting classes. In comparison, the African American students showed 64.1 percent truant (missing classes), with 12.8 percent "Often" and 51.3 percent "Sometimes," and 35.9 percent "Never." Latinos/Latinas had the lowest total rate at 60.0 percent of students cutting classes, with 9.1 percent "Often" and 50.9 percent "Sometimes."

Thus, while truancy is too high overall at 68.3 percent, the differences among ethnic groups is useful, with Whites at 87.1 percent truancy, African Americans at 64.1 percent, and Latinos/Latinas at 60 percent overall truancy from classes. These data, too, fly in the face of conventional wisdom that minority groups are the greatest truants when we see here that all groups are skipping out—but perhaps minorities are more likely to get caught. Kids do not cut because they're minorities. Perhaps in these schools, the Anglo-White kids thought they had "read" the system better and were absent from their classes more as a group.

Truancy by Level of "English Spoken at Home?"

A slightly different way to treat ethnicity as a point of analysis is to see if students with little or no English spoken in the home are less assimilated and perhaps more prone to be truant from school. This measure may also be an indicator of immigrant status—and the years the family has been in the United States of America and the degree to which schools are meeting the needs of these students.

Table 2.20 shows the level of school skipping cross-hatched by the predominant language of the home: no English spoken at all, some English spoken, or all English at home? The "No English" spoken at home group of students, although quite small in this sample (20 total, of which 2 cut "Often" and 11 "Sometimes') did show that 65 percent were truant. The "Some English" (and obviously some other language spoken) group had 13.3 percent skipping school "Often" and 86.7 percent of the truants missing "Sometimes." However, when compared to the total sample, only 35.7 percent (15 students out of a total "Some English" of 42 students) indicated being truant.

In the "Never" cut group, it appears that students from non-English-speaking families may attend a bit less: 35 percent attend for "No English" and 61.9 percent for "Some English," while "All English" had a high rate of attendance, with the "Never" cuts group at 63.1 attending (99 students out of a total "All English" sample of 156). See table 2.20, column 3, row 5. The significance level for English and non-English-speaking homes and school truancy was moderate at a Chi Square of 12.35 (d.f. = 6, p = .055).

Truancy by "Pretending" to Need Help in School

One clever way to get out of classes once at school, according to a STAR instrument item, is "pretending to need a nurse, a counselor, or to find a lost item" in the "lost and found." Using this technique, a student can sit in the nurse's office, complaining of headaches, cramps, an upset

Table 2.20. Truancy from School by Levels of English Spoken at Home

	No English	Some English	All English	Total
Often	2 (15.40%)	2 (13.3%)	16 (16.2%)	20 (23.3%)
Sometimes	11 (84.6%)	13 (86.7%)	42 (72.4%)	66 (76.7%)
Total Cuts	13 (65.0%)	15 (35.7%)	58 (36.9%)	86 (39.5%)
Never	7 (35.0%)	26 (61.9%)	99 (63.1%)	132 (60.5%)
Total Sample	20 (100%)	42 (100%)	156 (100%)	218 (100%)

stomach, when nothing is the matter, and not have to attend a class that day. Or, a student may seek counseling, taking up a class period or two making an appointment or attending a session with a guidance person.

Table 2.21 shows the rate of "pretending" by ethnic group. Interestingly, since the Asian group is so small and thus should be discounted for analytical purposes, the remaining groups were amazingly close in proportion in their use of a ploy to cut classes: the range is between Latino/Latina at 30.8 percent and Anglo-White at 36.7 percent, for an overall rate of pretending at 31.2 percent, as shown in table 2.21.

Furthermore, the differences among the groups on this scale were not significant on the Chi Square $= 1.34985$, d.f. $= 4$, p $= .8529$; nor was there a significant correlation between these variables as shown in a Pearson's R at $-.01293$ with p $= .4272$. Hence, our data on ethnic group variances show rather narrow ranges of difference among groups concerning students who plays hooky by telling little lies to cut class. About one-third of students in each of the ethno-cultural groups in this sample admitted that they had pretended to need help to escape a class.

Truancy to Where?

Another relevant question by ethnic group for those being truant from class is: Where do students go when they cut a teacher's class or activity? Do they leave the school property or remain "hidden" from class but stay on school property. In table 2.22, data show that overall, 42.1 percent of the students stayed in the building sometimes, 30.2 percent always stayed in the building when cutting their classes, and 27.7 percent left the building when playing hooky. The ranges are informative, with 37.8 percent of

Table 2.21. Incidence of Students Cutting Classes by "Pretending" to Need Help Falsely—by Ethnic Group

	African American	Latino/ Latina	Anglo White	Asian American	Other	Total Groups
Yes, Pretend	22 (31.0%)	16 (30.8%)	11 (36.7%)	2 (50.0%)	13 (27.7%)	65 (31.2%)
No, Not Pretend	49 (69.0%)	36 (69.2%)	19 (63.3%)	2 (50.0%)	34 (72.3%)	140 (68.6%)
Total Sample	71 (100%)	52 (100%)	30 (100%)	4 (100%)	47 (100%)	204 (100%)

Table 2.22. Cutting Class and Staying on School Property by Ethnicity
"Did you stay in the School Building?"

	African American	Latino/ Latina	Anglo White	Asian American	Other	Total Groups
1. Stay in Building Sometimes	21	15	16	2	13	67
% of Cuts	(39.6%)	(40.5%)	(59.3%)	(40.0%)	(35.1%)	(42.1%)
2. Always Stay in Building	19	15	3	1	10	48
	(35.9%)	(40.5%)	(11.1%)	(20.0%)	(27.0%)	(30.2%)
3. Left Building	13	7	8	2	14	44
	(24.5%)	(18.9%)	(29.6%)	(40.0%)	(37.8%)	(27.7%)
4. Total Cuts	53	37	27	5	37	159
% of Total	(68.8%)	(62.3%)	(90.0%)	(100%)	(75.5%)	(73.6%)
5. Did Not Cut	24	18	3	0	12	57
% of Total	(31.2%)	(32.7%)	(10.0%)	(0%)	(24.5%)	(26.4%)
6. Total Sample	77	55	30	5	49	216
	(100%)	(100%)	(100%)	(100%)	(100%)	(100%)

the "Other" student category saying that they left regularly, while the lowest group average of going off campus were the Latinos/Latinas at 18.9 percent, who preferred to stay on the school grounds or building. Among the "Sometimes" stayed students, the "Other" ethnic group was 35.1 percent, with the African Americans at 39.6 percent, Latinos/Latinas at 40.5 percent, and Anglo-Whites at 59.3 percent.

Thus, about 70 percent of students left their schools "sometimes" and "usually" when cutting, and 30.2 percent cut but stayed in the building (perhaps going to the nurse or lost and found, or lounging around the building). Latinos/Latinas tended to cut but remain around (40.5 percent indicated that they were always in the school when cutting), the most of these groups, while the Anglo-Whites were most likely to leave (only 11.1 percent admitted "Always" staying on premises).

Playing Truant with Whom? By Ethnic Group

Data were collected by ethnic group for both kinds of truant students and with whom they cut school and class. Table 2.23 shows that Anglo-White students were likely to stay away from school with friends at (61.5%), while African American students at 78.8 percent and Latinos

Table 2.23. Cutting School With Whom? by Ethnic Group

	African American	Latino/ Latina	Anglo White	Asian American	Other	Total Groups
Cutting Alone	7	5	5	2	11	30
	(21.2%)	(21.7%)	(38.5%)	(40.0%)	(42.3%)	(30.0%)
Cutting with Friends	26	18	8	3	15	70
	(78.8%)	(78.3%)	(61.5%)	(60.0%)	(57.7%)	(70.0%)
Total Cutting	33	23	13	5	26	100
	(45.2%)	(42.6%)	(44.8%)	(100%)	(53.1%)	(47.6%)
Non-Cutters	40	31	16	0	23	110
	(54.8%)	(57.4%)	(55.2%)	(0%)	(46.9%)	(52.4%)
Total Sample	73	54	29	5	49	210
	(100%)	(100%)	(100%)	(100%)	(100%)	(100%)

at 78.3 percent more frequently were truant in groups. Overall, for all ethnic groups, only 30 percent cut alone, reinforcing the "social" side of the truancy equation.

When looking at missing selective classes (post-registration truancy), as shown in table 2.24, we find exactly the same level of cutting alone for both kinds of truancy: 30.1 percent for skipping classes alone and 30.4 percent for being absent alone from school without a valid excuse. Asians and Whites cut classes with friends at a lower rate of 60.0 percent and 63 percent compared to African Americans at 79.3 percent and Latinos at

Table 2.24. Cutting Class With Whom? by Ethnic Group

	African American	Latino/ Latina	Anglo White	Asian American	Other	Total Groups
Cutting Alone % of Cuts	11	11	10	2	14	48
	(20.8%)	(33.3%)	(37.0%)	(40.0%)	(36.8%)	(30.2%)
Cutting with Friends	42	25	17	3	24	111
	(79.3%)	(69.4%)	(63.0%)	(60.0%)	(63.2%)	(69.8%)
Total Cutting % of Total	53	36	27	5	38	159
	(68.8%)	(65.5%)	(87.1%)	(100%)	(73.1%)	(72.3%)
Non-Cutters	24	19	4	0	14	161
	(31.2%)	(34.5%)	(12.9%)	(0%)	(26.9%)	(73.2%)
Total Sample	77	55	31	5	52	220
	(100%)	(100%)	(100%)	(100%)	(100%)	(100%)

69.4 percent. Again, these data on cutting classes, like that on missing school, support the group quality of missing school with 69.8 percent.

Truancy and Getting Caught by Ethnic Group

Another indicator of diligence on the part of school authorities is the percent of students stating that they "got caught" for cutting once or more than once, or conversely that they cut and didn't get apprehended by school authorities. Table 2.25 shows the "getting caught" percentage for cutting class. It breaks out the data into four "Cut" categories ("Cut and Caught More Often," "Cut and Caught Once," "Cut but Not Caught," and "Total Cutters"). Then, to complete the analysis, we include the "Never Cuts" to make up the full sample of 215 students who answered this question on STAR.

When asked about being "Caught Often" for cutting classes, the Anglo-Whites in the sample were highest at 31.2 percent of those cutting and being caught. Next came African Americans (with the small Asian sample

Table 2.25. Classroom Truancy and Frequency of Students' "Getting Caught"

Class Truancy	African American	Latino/ Latina	Anglo/ White	Asian American	Other	All Groups
Cut and Caught Often	8	2	10	4	9	33
% of Truants	(17.0%)	(6.4%)	(31.2%)	(80.0%)	(25.7%)	(22.9%)
Cut and Caught Once	14	7	6	0	11	38
% of Truants	(29.8%)	(22.6%)	(18.8%)	(0%)	(31.4%)	(26.4%)
Cut but Not Caught	25	22	16	1	15	73
% of Truants	(53.2%)	(71.0%)	(50.0%)	(20.0%)	(42.9%)	(50.7%)
Total Cutters	47	31	32	5	35	144
% of Total	(62.7%)	(65.4%)	(88.9%)	(100%)	(70.0%)	(67.0%)
Never Cut	28	24	4	0	15	71
% of Total	(37.3%)	(43.6%)	(11.1%)	(0%)	(30.0%)	(33.0%)
Total Sample	75	55	36	5	50	215
	(100%)	(100%)	(100%)	(100%)	(100%)	(100%)

at 80 percent and the others at 25.7 percent). Lowest were the Latino/ Latinas in the sample with only 6.4 percent getting caught often for skipping classes. The average for "All Groups" being "Caught Often" was 22.9 percent or 33 students out of the sample of truants of 144 in this sample.

Next came the "Caught Once" group: here the African American students recorded 29.8 percent, Latinos at 22.6 percent, and Whites at 18.8 percent, with the total of those truant averaging 26.4 percent for all ethnic groups together. Most interesting, perhaps, are the large numbers of students who cut and escape undetected by school authorities — and these students are presumably checked into the school and are cutting during the school day. Overall, among the 144 cutters, 73 or 50.7 percent were never caught at all. That means that of the 67 percent of students reporting that they cut classes, about half of them were never once apprehended.

Of the ethnic groups, Latinos/Latinas were most skillful at cutting and not getting caught, with their average "Not Caught" running 71.0 percent; next came the African Americans with 53.2 percent not caught, and Anglo-Whites at 50.0 percent. Other had 42.9 percent never caught. Finally, the "Never Cut" in the first place cohort average about a third (33.0 percent) of the total sample.

The Latino group was doubly endowed: it cut less (43.6 percent never cut at all) and it was "Not Caught" at a rate of 71 percent. When one combines the Latino truancy rate (65.4 percent) in this sample with their ability to get away with it, this group had the lowest "Caught" ratio in the study: only 29 percent were caught as truants, while 51 percent of Whites and 47 percent of African Americans were nabbed at least once. Overall, "crime pays," or so it seems, as only half of the truancy group were never caught once, among the two-thirds of the students who are truant from classes.

Truancy: School Telling Parents/Guardians, by Student Ethnicity

Of the 55.1 percent of students who skipped school overall (or 113 out of the 205 respondents in this survey), only 42 or 37.2 percent said that the school called their home. We then analyzed the tell/no telling the home by ethnic identification. See table 2.26. Even though Latinos had a comparatively lower rate of school truancy, their rate of home notification by authorities was the highest at 51.9 percent, meaning that about 48 percent reported being nabbed but no home phone call or letter occurred. The

Table 2.26. **Reported School Truancy to the Home by Ethnic/Racial Group**

Parents/Home told or not of cutting school:

	African American	Latino/ Latina	Anglo White	Asian American	Other	All Groups
Caught—						
School Told	13	14	4	2	9	42
Home	(34.2%)	(51.9%)	(25.0%)	(40.0%)	(33.3%)	(37.2%)
Caught—	25	13	12	3	18	71
Not Told	(65.8)	(48.1%)	(75.0%)	(60.0%)	(66.7%)	(62.8%)
Total Truants	38	27	16	5	27	113
	(53.5%)	(51.9%)	(55.2%)	(100%)	(56.3%)	(55.1%)
Non-Truants	33	25	13	0	21	92
	(46.5%)	(48.1%)	(44.8%)	(0%)	(43.7%)	(44.9%)
Total Sample	71	52	29	5	48	205
	(100%)	(100%)	(100%)	(100%)	(100%)	(100%)

African American students came next, with 34.2 percent finding their parents/guardians called, with Anglo-Whites at 25 percent, and Other at 33.3 percent. Overall, the average notification rate for the whole sample across ethnic groups was 37.2 percent. Thus, out of the entire survey sample of 205 students who answered this question, 55.1 percent were truant. Of that subgroup of 113 students, only 42 pupils or 37.2 percent of the cutters had homes notified that they were absent from school at all, at least according to the students.

Truancy: School Punishment by Student Ethnicity

The final step in the truancy process is whether to punish offenders or not: this decision, of course, depends on the school having set a policy, caught a student, and usually notified the home. Often, too, students are rounded up in groups since group skipping and cutting are so common. Table 2.27 shows the results of students' reporting on whether they are punished, segmented by the ethnicity of the students. Three choice are considered: "Caught, But Not Punished," "Caught and Punished," "Non-Truants."

The analysis here includes those students who (a) cut class and (b) were caught and (c) were or (d) were not punished. We did not consider in this table those students who cut and were not caught (we covered that contingency above). Overall, about 32 percent of students caught were actually

Table 2.27. School Punishment Rates for Cutting Classes by Ethnic Group

	African American	Latino/ Latina	Anglo- White	Asian American	Other	All Groups
Caught—						
But Not Punished	33 (73.3%)	22 (51.9%)	15 (57.7%)	2 (40.0%)	26 (74.3%)	98 (67.6%)
Caught— And Punished	12 (26.7%)	12 (35.3%)	11 (42.4%)	3 (60.0%)	9 (25.7%)	47 (32.4%)
Total Truants % of Total	45 (64.3%)	34 (65.4%)	26 (89.7%)	5 (100%)	35 (68.6%)	145 (70.0%)
Non-Truants % of Total	25 (35.7%)	18 (34.6%)	3 (10.3%)	0 (0%)	16 (31.4%)	62 (30.0%)
Total Sample	70 (100%)	52 (100%)	29 (100%)	5 (100%)	51 (100%)	207 (100%)

punished, as reported by the students themselves of the STAR survey. When separated by ethnicity, Anglo-White students reported that 42.4 percent were punished (the Asians were higher but only five students appeared in the sample). The African American and other ethnic groups reported lower levels of punishments, with only 26.7 percent of the African-American students and 25.7 percent of the "Other" students admitting to being punished. Thus, of the total students caught, measuring about 70 percent, about 68 percent were let go and 32.4 percent were punished.

3. Truancy and Academic Standing

Academic standing is another useful way to examine the cutting and skipping data, as well as the consequences. Are the "better" academic pupils absent less often for unacceptable reasons? Is the school less likely to take strong action in catching these truants, informing their parents, and punishing them severely—since "these are our best pupils"? Conversely, do low-attaining kids skip more? Or, perhaps the causality runs both ways: the poor performers are more disenchanted and less engaged; or the high cutters and skippers earn their low academic standing because they miss more lessons, activities, tests, and extra help.

Data in this section relate the truancy of students to their perception of their academic progress: Excellent (A/B+), Good (B/B−), Fair (C/D), and Poor (D−/F). It covers the same set of behaviors: being truant, where, with whom, getting caught, home notification, and punishment.

As shown in table 2.28, the students with higher reported academic standing cut less than those at the middle and lower end, although very few (only four) students admitted to having a failing average, and 38 were "fair" (C/D). Among those cutting "Often," the best students were 6.3 percent, "Good" were 12.5 percent cutting class, "Fair" were 21.1 percent, and "Poor" were 75 percent, indicating a strong relationship between academic standing and cutting often.

However, the occasional cutters seemed less related to academics, with the A/B+ students at 56.3 percent cutting "Sometimes," 56.7 percent for the "Good" (B/B−) students, and 52.6 percent for the "Fair" students. Thus, cutting once in a while seems unrelated to academic attainment.

The "Never" cut group was slightly skewed toward the upper end, with 37.5 percent of the A/B+ students admitting to having never cut. By the "Fair" and "Poor" students (N = 1), the percent dropped to around 25 percent. Thus, those students who chronically cut class are more likely to do poorly or fair in their grades, although it is impossible to tell which way the causality is running: Are students staying away from class because they are not achieving? Or are they achieving below par because they do not come to class regularly? We cannot tell from these data, but one can assume that both forces are at work. That is, students miss school and do

Table 2.28. Cutting Class Segmented by Students' Self-Reported Grades

	"Excellent" (A/B+)	"Good" (B/B−)	"Fair" (C/D)	"Poor" (D−/F)	All Grades
1. Cut Class Often	4 (6.3%)	15 (12.5%)	8 (21.1%)	3 (75%)	30 (13.2%)
2. Cut Class Sometimes	36 (56.3%)	68 (56.7%)	20 (52.6%)	0 (0%)	124 (54.9%)
3. Cut Class Never	24 (37.5%)	37 (30.8%)	10 (26.3%)	1 (25%)	72 (31.9%)
Total Sample	64 (100%)	120 (100%)	38 (100%)	4 (100%)	226 (100%)

badly; then they do even worse by missing classes, assignments, tests, and other opportunities to learn.

School Truancy by Academic Achievement

Table 2.29 indicates a continuous rise of students' cutting school often by grade achievements. When asked about cutting "Often," the "Excellent" students report 9.7 percent; "Good" students claim 4.4 percent; "Fair" students indicate 16.2 percent; and "Poor" students record 80 percent, for a total of 9.2 percent for all students (grades A to F). A similar increase occurs for students who cut "Sometimes," with "Excellent" students cutting 25.8 percent; "Good" students cutting 33.0 percent; and "Fair" students cutting 32.4 percent.

With all the cutters ("Often" and "Sometimes") combined, the "Excellent" students showed 35.5 percent being truant from school; 37.4 percent of the "Good" students and 48.7 percent of the "Fair" students missed school for an unsanctioned reason; 80 percent of those with "Poor" grades, though the sample is small, and overall, cutting school was admitted to by 39.5 percent or 86 of the 218 sample pupils in this study.

To test the significance of the average "School Truancy by Achievement Level" of students, we found a Chi Square of 28.38 (d.f. = 0) at $p < .0008$, meaning that grades were a significant difference between

Table 2.29.   School Truancy by Achievement Level

	"Excellent" (A/B+)	"Good" (B/B−)	"Fair" (C/D)	"Poor" (D−/F)	All Grades
Cut School Often	6 (9.7%)	5 (4.4%)	6 (16.2%)	4 (80.0%)	20 (9.2%)
Cut School Sometimes	16 (25.8%)	38 (33.0%)	12 (32.4%)	0 (0%)	66 (30.3%)
Cutters Total: % of Total:	22 (35.5%)	43 (37.4%)	18 (48.7%)	4 (80.0%)	86 (39.5%)
Cut School Never % of Total:	40 (64.5%)	72 (62.6%)	19 (51.4%)	1 (20.0%)	132 (60.6%)
Total Sample	62 (100%)	115 (100%)	37 (100%)	5 (100%)	218 (100%)

the actual and predicted scores. A test of the relationship between grades in school and truancy was explored using a Pearson's R, which was −.154 (p < .011).

Cutting Class to Where? By Academic Achievement

Table 2.30 reports 73.9 percent of the students with grades ranging from excellent (A) to poor (failing) cutting class. A break out by academic achievement indicates that the "Excellent" students cut 64.5 percent. Of those brighter students, 50 percent "sometimes left the school building" when they cut class, while 27.5 percent "always left the school building" and 22.5 percent cut class but remained in the building.

Of a student reporting "good" (B/B−) grades, a total of 73.5 percent cut class with 29 percent claiming that they always left the building, 34.9 percent stating they sometimes left the premise, and 36.1 percent reporting they remained in the building. Students with "Fair" to "Poor" grades show higher incidence of cutting class, with average students reporting 88.6 percent who claimed to leave the building "Sometimes." In fact, when we ran a Chi Square (27.02, d.f. = 9, p ≤ .0014) and Pearson's R (.15, p ≤ .0120) on the data, we found significance. Clearly, these findings raise legal and ethical questions for administrators and teachers who are entrusted

Table 2.30. Cutting Class to Where? By Students' Self-Reported Grades

	"Excellent" A/B+	*"Good"* B/B−	*"Fair"* C/D	*"Poor"* D−/F	*All* Grades
Cut, Left Building Sometimes	20 (50.0%)	30 (34.9%)	17 (54.8%)	1 (25.0%)	68 (42.2%)
Cut, Left Building Always	11 (27.5%)	25 (29.0%)	12 (38.7%)	0 (0%)	48 (29.8%)
Cut, Did Not Leave Building	9 (22.5%)	31 (36.1%)	2 (6.5%)	3 (75.0%)	45 (28.0%)
Total Cut	40 (64.5%)	86 (73.5%)	31 (88.6%)	4 (100%)	161 (73.9%)
Did Not Cut	22 (35.5%)	31 (26.5%)	4 (11.5%)	0 (0%)	57 (26.1%)
Total Sample	62 (100%)	117 (100%)	35 (100%)	4 (100%)	218 (100%)

with the care and safety of students. Although "excellent" and "good" students are arriving to school, a combined total of 58.6 percent them "disappear" right in the building.

Being Punished for Cutting Class by Academic Achievement

Table 2.31 reports a total of 70 percent of students with grades of Excellent (A/B+) to Poor (D−/F) cutting class. In examining grades and the use of punishment when students cut class, we found some interesting patterns. "Excellent" students reported cutting class and *not* being punished 83.8 percent of the time. "Good" students, achieving a B average, reported cutting and not being punished 67.5 percent of time, while only 50.0 percent of the students with "Fair" grades reported cutting class without any sanction. These findings raise questions about schools showing preferential treatment for their "better" students and punishing more frequently those below average.

Of the bright ("Excellent") students, 16.2 percent claimed they cut and were punished; "Good" students reported cutting and being punished 32.5 percent of the time; 50.7 percent of the "Fair" students and 75 percent of the poor students reported cutting and being punished. When we ran a Chi Square, we found high levels of significance (28.38 d.f.= 9, p ≤ .0002) for the predicted versus the actual truancy values by student achievement levels. The relationship between the variables of student academic achievement and cutting classes was Pearson's R = .25 p ≤ .0008.

Table 2.31. Punishment for Cutting Class by Academic Achievement Level

Class	"Excellent" A/B+	"Good" B/B−	"Fair" C/D	"Poor" D−/F	All Grades
Cut, Not Punished	31 (83.8%)	54 (67.5%)	13 (50.0%)	1 (25.0%)	99 (67.3%)
Cut and Punished		2 (32.5%)	13 (50.7%)	3 (75.0%)	48 (32.7%)
Total Cutting Class	37 (62.7%)	80 (70.2%)	26 (78.8%)	4 (100%)	147 (70.0%)
Not Cuts	22 (37.3%)	34 (29.8%)	7 (21.2%)	0 (0%)	63 (30.0%)
Total Sample	59 (100%)	114 (100%)	33 (100%)	4 (100%)	210 (100%)

4. Truancy and Grade Level

If we assume that truancy is a learned behavior, one done with some care and consideration, then perhaps students "get better at reading the system" the longer they are in the school. Or perhaps truancy increases as students figure out the process: where to cut, with whom, when, and how often.

This section segments the truancy process by the grade level, starting at age fourteen with the eighth grade, through age eighteen with grade twelve. This longitudinal quality, taking in students across five grade levels, gives some sense of the "learning curve," particularly if the entry level students, grade eight, are less likely to be truant than the older students in the upper grades. Other factors enter in as well: older students have more knowledge of the community and more mobility. Older students may also have amassed poor habits in school (staying up late, doing less homework and studying) and these affect their likelihood of attending school or class. If a student is behind academically in the eighth grade, this condition may be exacerbated over the next four years, with the student falling further and further behind with each passing year. Thus, the incentive to be truant rises as the stake in school success diminishes.

Again, we apply the standard behaviors (being truant, alone or with friends, on or off the school grounds, getting caught, parents told, and punishment applied). We seek to learn if the maturing process, captured by the passing of the grade levels, has any impact on students and their coming to school and classes.

Cutting Class by Grade Level

Table 2.32, for example, separates the "cutting class" behavior among the given grade levels, eighth through twelfth, indicating a general rise in truancy as students rise in grade levels. As shown, only one eighth grader admitted to cutting "Often" while by 12th grade the percentage was 19.6 percent or 30 students. cutting "Sometimes" showed 14 students at the eighth grade out of a total eighth-grade cohort of 26 students or 53.9 percent; by the senior year, the percent cutting "Sometimes" was at 65 percent or 26 out of a total of 40. And when we examine "Total Cuts" (table 2.32, row 3), we note a dramatic growth in cutting behaviors, from 36.6 percent at eighth grade to 87.5 percent (35 out a total cutters of 40). Since the item was phrased "In the last few years, have you cut class? Often,

Table 2.32.   Truancy from Class by Students' Grade Level, 8th–12th

	8th Grade	9th Grade	10th Grade	11th Grade	12th Grade	All Grades
1. Cuts Sometimes	14	24	44	15	26	123
	(93.3%)	(88.9%)	(72.1%)	(100%)	(74.3%)	(80.4%)
2. Cuts Often	1	3	17	0	9	30
	(6.7%)	(11.1%)	(27.9%)	(0%)	(25.7%)	(19.6%)
3. Total Cuts	15	27	61	15	35	153
	(36.6%)	(62.8%)	(74.4%)	(75.0%)	(87.5%)	(67.7%)
4. Never Cuts	26	16	21	5	5	73
	(63.4%)	(37.2%)	(25.6%)	(25.0%)	(12.5%)	(32.3%)
5. Total Sample by Grade	41	43	82	20	40	226
	(100%)	(100%)	(100%)	(100%)	(100%)	(100%)

Sometimes, Never," we assume that being truant from class had become a fairly common practice year by year.

This growth in truancy gives some credence to several theories of cause: perhaps students became wiser and more canny, learning the ropes and figuring out how to cut class repeatedly. Or perhaps by the twelfth grade, students were sufficiently bored with class, as Stoll and O'Keeffe (1989) found in England, to cut out when they felt the need, for almost 88 percent of students were cutting by the end of their school career, compared to just 37 percent in the eighth grade.

School Truancy by Years in the School

Another measure of students' involvement in their school is the time spent there: Are they new or have they been in the building for a number of years? Is truancy affected by being new or a veteran? Table 2.33 reports the total percent of students who cut school "Sometimes" and who have been in school for one to five years at 76.7 percent. Students in their first year are the highest cutters, reporting "Sometimes" cutting school 88.2 percent. By the time students reach the fourth year, we see a drop in cutting school "Sometimes" to 62.5 percent and in remarkable rise in fifth-year students to 80 percent. If these data are reliable, one might conclude that the first year is a great temptation, and that by the fifth year (for students who likely have been retained or failed), the truancy may reoccur.

Table 2.33.   Cutting School by Years in School

	1 Year	2 Years	3 Years	4 Years	5 Years	Total All
Often	2	6	4	6	2	20
	(11.8%)	(23.1%)	(23.5%)	(37.5%)	(20.0%)	(23.3%)
Sometimes	15	20	13	10	8	66
	(88.2%)	(76.9%)	(76.5%)	(62.5%)	(80.0%)	(76.7%)
Total Cuts	17	26	17	16	10	86
	(33.3%)	(36.6%)	(33.3%)	(61.5%)	(47.6%)	(39.5%)
Never	33	45	34	10	11	33
	(66.7%)	(63.4%)	(66.7%)	(38.5%)	(52.4%)	(60.7%)
Total Sample	51	71	51	26	21	219
	(100%)	(100%)	(100%)	(100%)	(100%)	(100%)

In analyzing the results of frequent cutting ("Often") school, we see a steady rise with first-year students reporting cutting school "Often," at 11.8 percent; second-year students, 23.1 percent; third-year, 23.5 percent; and a dramatic rise for fourth-year students at 37.5 percent. Although, fifth-year students report "Sometimes" cutting at 80 percent, they report cutting "Often" only 20 percent of the time. When measuring the actual truancy levels by years attending the particular school, the results are not significant (Chi Square = 14.93, d.f. = 12, p = .255).

School Truancy by Grade Level

As shown in Table 2.34, cutting school went up fairly consistently with the increase in grade levels. Hence, eighth graders were truant from school 22.5 percent of the time (column 3, row 1), ninth graders at 34.2 percent cutting, tenth graders with 38.0 percent, eleventh with 50 percent, and twelfth graders, 55.0 percent, for a total across the grade levels (eighth through twelfth) at 38.6 percent.

When the data are broken out by "Sometimes" and "Often" cuts, the "Often" truants from school also went up steadily by grade: eighth grade with 22.2 percent; ninth with 21.4 percent; tenth with 26.7 percent, and twelfth with 31.8 percent, for a 23.5 percent of the cutters cutting often. This shows a kind of learning curve; it also may indicate greater mobility with eleventh and twelfth graders able to "travel" more freely on their own (slip into the folk's BMW and you're away!). Whatever the cause, with time in school

Table 2.34. School Truancy by Grade Level

	8th Grade	9th Grade	10th Grade	11th Grade	12th Grade	All Grades
Cut School Sometimes	7 (77.8%)	11 (78.6%)	22 (73.3%)	10 (100%)	15 (68.2%)	65 (76.5%)
Cut School Often	2 (22.2%)	3 (21.4%)	8 (26.7%)	0 (0%)	7 (31.8%)	20 (23.5%)
Total Cuts	9 (22.5%)	14 (34.2%)	30 (38.0%)	10 (50.0%)	22 (55.0%)	85 (38.6%)
Never Cut School	31 (41.5%)	27 (65.9%)	49 (62.0%)	10 (50.0%)	18 (45.0%)	135 (61.4%)
Total Sample	40 (100%)	41 (100%)	79 (100%)	20 (100%)	40 (100%)	220 (100%)

comes greater distraction, perhaps boredom, perhaps a figuring out of the system, and truancy goes up with each grade level.

When tests of significance were applied we find a moderate Chi Square of 20.08 (d.f. = 12) p = .07 and a relationship between grade level and truancy using the Pearson's R of .187 (p = .005).

Cutting Class to Where—by Grade Level

Analysis examined the pattern of "where" students were truant from class, whether "Always" staying in the school building, "Sometimes" staying, Generally leaving the building, or Not cutting at all. Table 2.35 displays data by grade level and location patterns of being truant from class. As is obvious, the "Always Stayed in Building" declined markedly between eighth grade at 58.8 percent to only 5.7 percent by twelfth grade. Students apparently gain confidence and knowledge, wandering farther from school as they matured. This gives credence to the notion that truancy is a learned, rational behavior associated with growth, not the purview of some troubled youth.

Table 2.35, row 1, shows those simply leaving the building as a matter of course, rising from 17.7 percent in the eighth grade to 34.3 percent by the twelfth grade. And the "Sometimes Stayed" went from 23.5 percent in eighth to 60.0 percent by the eleventh and twelfth grades. Overall, for all grades, the breakout between leavers and those in favor of clearing out:

Table 2.35. **Location of Cutting Classes by Grade Level**

	8th Grade	9th Grade	10th Grade	11th Grade	12th Grade	All Grades
1. Left School Building	3	10	18	3	12	46
% of Cuts	(17.7%)	(30.3%)	(29.5%)	(20.0%)	(34.3%)	(28.6%)
2. Sometimes Stayed	4	13	21	9	21	68
in Building	(23.5%)	(39.4%)	(34.4%)	(60.0%)	(60.0%)	(42.2%)
3. Always Stayed	10	10	22	3	2	47
in Building	(58.8%)	(30.3%)	(36.1%)	(20.0%)	(5.7%)	(29.2%)
4. Total Truants	17	33	61	15	35	161
% of Total	(41.5%)	(78.6%)	(79.2%)	(75.0%)	(87.5%)	(73.2%)
5. Did Not Cut	24	9	16	5	5	59
	(58.5%)	(21.4%)	(20.8%)	(25.0%)	(12.5%)	(26.8%)
6. Total Sample	41	42	77	20	40	220
	(100%)	(100%)	(100%)	(100%)	(100%)	(100%)

70.8 percent or 114 out of 161 students who cut at all, compared to just 29.2 percent who "Always stayed."

When we ran a test of significance on these inter-grade differences, we found the Chi Square at 47.03677, with d.f. = 12, and Significance at .0001. The Pearson's R was p = .26922, also Significant at .0001, showing that indeed staying and leaving were significantly different when considered by grade level and thus by age and maturity. Cutting class is very likely a learned behavior, not some trait or quality associated with some students and not others. In fact, as shown in table 2.35, row 5, only about 27 percent of the students indicated that they did not cut at all.

Incidence of Students' Cutting Classes by "Pretending" to Need Help, by Grade Level

Table 2.36 reveals that 31.6 percent of the students surveyed admitted to cutting class by pretending to need help from the school nurse, the guidance counselor, or by pretending to find a lost item. Eighth graders reported cutting class by pretending the least, only 9.1 percent of the time. However, the frequency increased to 16.7 percent for ninth graders and to 34.8 percent for tenth graders. We find eleventh graders reporting cutting class by pretending only 13.6 percent of the time, although this level may be a factor of

Table 2.36. Cutting Class—Pretending to Need Help by Grade Level

	8th Grade	9th Grade	10th Grade	11th Grade	12th Grade	All Grades
Yes, Pretend	6	11	23	9	17	66
	(9.1%)	(16.7%)	(34.8%)	(13.6%)	(25.8%)	(31.6%)
No, Not Pretend	30	30	51	10	22	143
	(21.0%)	(21.0%)	(35.7%)	(7.0%)	(15.4%)	(68.4%)
Total	36	41	74	19	39	209

a small sample size for this grade level. Seniors report, however, cutting 25.8 percent, suggesting a rise of pretending as students advance in grade level. Testing for significance, we found only moderate levels for Chi Square (8.94, $p \leq .063$) but greater significance for Pearson's (.20, $p \leq .002$).

1. Caught Cutting Class by Grade Level

Cut but Never Caught

As shown in table 2.37, of the eighth graders who cut class, 83.3 percent were "never caught," while among the seniors, 40.6 percent were *not*

Table 2.37. Frequency of Students Cutting Class and Getting Caught by Grade Level

	8th Grade	9th Grade	10th Grade	11th Grade	12th Grade	All Grades
1. Cut and Caught						
Often	0	1	18	2	12	33
% of Cuts	(0%)	(3.5%)	(29.0%)	(13.3%)	(37.5%)	(22.6%)
2. Cut and Caught	2	13	16	4	7	38
Once	(16.7%)	(44.8%)	(25.8%)	(26.7%)	(21.9%)	(26.0%)
Total Cut and Caught	2	14	34	6	19	71
% of Total Truants	(16.7%)	(48.3%)	(54.8%)	(40.0%)	(59.4%)	(48.6%)
3. Cut—Never Caught	10	15	28	9	13	75
	(83.3%)	(51.7%)	(45.2%)	(60.0%)	(40.6%)	(51.4%)
% of Total Truants	100%	100%	100%	100%	100%	100%
4. Total Truants	12	29	62	15	32	146
% of Total	(31.6%)	(61.7%)	(77.5%)	(75.0%)	(82.1%)	(66.4%)
5. Did Not Cut	26	18	18	5	7	74
% of Total	(68.4%)	(38.3%)	(22.5%)	(25.0%)	(17.9%)	(33.6%)
Total Sample	38	47	80	20	39	220
	(100%)	(100%)	(100%)	(100%)	(100%)	(100%)

nabbed for being out of class without an acceptable reason. In between, the ninth graders recorded 51.7 percent Never Caught and tenth graders, 45.2 percent (eleventh grade was eliminated for small sample size).

Cut and Caught OFTEN

When breaking out "Cut and Caught Often," however, we see small numbers but again a fairly regular increase with grade levels: 8th grade at 0 percent, ninth = 3.5 percent; tenth = 29 percent; eleventh = 13.3 percent; and twelfth grade, 37.5 percent, with the overall "Cut and Caught" rate at 22.6 percent for the cutters! If one includes all the students, cutters and non-cutters, then the percent "Caught Often" is much lower at 15 percent (33 out of the 220 students total).

Cut and Caught ONCE

And for "Cut and Caught Once," we see the percentage of apprehended truants for the lower grades at 16.7 percent (eighth grade), 44.8 percent (ninth grade), 25.8 percent (tenth grade), 26.7 percent (eleventh grade), and 21.9 percent (twelfth grade), for a total of 26 percent being "Caught Once" who were cutters.

Total Truant and Caught

The total of those students who were truant *and* caught by grade looks like this: eighth grade at 16.7 percent, ninth at 48.3 percent, tenth grade at 54.8 percent, eleventh = 40 percent, and twelfth = 59.4 percent, for a total "Caught" level of 48.6 percent of all cutters and 32.3 percent of the total sample: 71 students out of 220.

Yet, the truancy rate itself goes up with grade levels: that is, eighth graders "Did Not Cut" at the eighth-grade level at 68.4 percent, ninth graders at 38.3 percent, 22.5 percent of the tenth grade, eleventh grade 25 percent, and seniors 17.9 percent. The effects, then, of grade level are twofold. First, the *truancy* rate rises by grade level from 32 percent to 82 percent, second, the percent of students *caught* also rises, although less strongly: from 16.7 percent in eighth grade to 59.4 percent in twelfth grade.

Thus, while this sample shows 146 out of 220 students (66.4 percent) admitting to cutting classes, only 71 students (48.6 percent) were actually caught and 75 were not. It appears that administrators and teachers may be overlooking the early adolescent behavior of their eighth-grade students; or perhaps the middle school that these students attend is more lax in rounding up the transgressors than the more hard-nosed high schools where 60 of the seniors were caught, without an acceptable reason. (See table 2.37.)

Telling Parents/Guardians of School Truancy by Student Grade Level

As shown in table 2.38, school administration informed the home about children's cutting *school* at an overall rate of 42.1 percent. However, when broken out by grade level, no clear pattern emerges. For example, the lower grades were above the average, with eighth graders' reporting 46.2 percent and ninth, 53.6 percent (average was 42.1 percent).

Then in the middle grades, we see an apparent drop to 37.7 percent at tenth grade and a remarkable dip, 18.8 percent at eleventh grade, although this anomaly may be a factor of unusually small sample size (if only 3 students whose parents were told and 13 students whose parents were not). But at twelfth grade, the school informed the home of truancy 50 percent of the time. Thus, although cutting school rose steadily from eighth graders at 32.5 percent to twelfth graders at 85.0 percent, the practice of telling parents about school truancy was quite erratic for reasons not clear to us. Significance levels were extremely high for both the Chi Square (43.83, d.f. = 12, $p \leq .0001$) and Pearson's R (.29, $p \leq .0001$).

Table 2.38. "Telling Parents" about Cutting School by Grade Level

School	8th Grade	9th Grade	10th Grade	11th Grade	12th Grade	All Grades
Cut—Told Parents	6 (46.2%)	15 (53.6%)	23 (37.7%)	3 (18.8%)	17 (50.0%)	64 (42.1%)
Cut—Not Told Parents	7 (53.8%)	13 (46.4%)	38 (62.3%)	13 (81.2%)	17 (50.0%)	88 (57.9%)
Total Cuts	13 (32.5%)	28 (68.3%)	61 (75.3%)	16 (80.0%)	34 (85.0%)	152 (68.5%)
No Cutting	27 (67.5%)	13 (31.7%)	20 (24.7%)	4 (20.0%)	6 (15.0%)	70 (31.5%)
Total Sample	40 (100%)	41 (100%)	81 (100%)	20 (100%)	40 (100%)	222 (100%)

Getting Punished for Cutting Class by Grade Level

Table 2.39 reports that a total of 67.8 percent of the students in grades eight through twelve cut class without any consequences for their behavior. While the overall significance of cutting class by grade level tested at p ≤ .0002 (suggesting a significant rise of class cutters not being punished), we also noted a distinct pattern when grade levels were analyzed. Eighth graders report cutting class and not being punished 64.3 percent of the time. By ninth grade, that number increased significantly (Chi Square = 30.33, d.f.= 8, p ≤ .0002; with a significant relationship: Pearson's R = .28, p ≤ .001) to 76.0 percent, with an unusual drop occurring among tenth graders, who reported cutting class without sanctions 65.0 percent of the time.

Then we note a dramatic rise of juniors' cutting class without punishment, a record of 85.7 percent of the time. However, the small sample size of juniors may account for this anomaly. Seniors report cutting class without sanctions 60.6 percent of the time. The findings indicate that cutting class is on a steady rise with eighth graders reporting 36.8 percent to twelfth graders reporting 86.8 percent.

However, even more disturbing news is noted with the younger students in eighth and ninth grades cutting class at high rates without consequences. With prior truancy being the best predictor of future truancy, this finding should alert administrators to issues of transition from middle schools to high schools.

Table 2.39. Being Punished for Cutting Class by Grade Level

	8th Grade	9th Grade	10th Grade	11th Grade	12th Grade	All Grades
Cut Class, Punished	5 (35.7%)	6 (24.0%)	21 (35.0%)	2 (14.3%)	13 (39.4%)	47 (32.2%)
Cut Class, Not Punished	9 (64.3%)	19 (76.0%)	39 (65.0%)	12 (85.7%)	20 (60.6%)	99 (67.8%)
Total Cutters	14 (36.8%)	25 (67.7%)	60 (75.9%)	14 (73.7%)	33 (86.8%)	146 (69.2%)
Did Not Cut	24 (63.2%)	12 (32.4%)	19 (24.1%)	5 (26.3%)	5 (13.2%)	65 (30.8%)
Total Sample	38 (100%)	37 (100%)	79 (100%)	19 (100%)	38 (100%)	221 (100%)

5. Truancy and School Rules

Another assumption to be tested in this research is the perception by students of school rules and regulations affecting their attending or non-attending school and class. The environment in which students make their personal truant decisions is critical; perhaps schools, districts, and teachers with clearly stated rules on skipping school and cutting class, with firm but fair enforcement, and with real consequences for these actions may place pressure on students to attend and have low truancy rates.

If we accept the notion that each student goes through a mental calculus: "Should I stay home from school today? Who will find out? Will I get caught and into trouble? Will I miss something in Mrs. Robinson's class that is exciting, worthwhile, important to my grade? Do I really want another hour today of boring Mr. Hogan's lecture on the mating life of the jar fly?

The relationship between rules and truancy is complex and difficult to analyze. In this study, we gave students a series of statements about rules in their schools and asked their reaction: Agree Strongly to Disagree Strongly: "My school has strict rules about cutting class." "If you cut class, the rules say that you will get into trouble." "My school has no written rules or policies on cutting." "If you cut class or school, you have to make up all the work." "Rules are clear and students follow them." These items were then rolled into a "My School's Rules" measure that allows us to correlate the scores with other sub-scales.

Perhaps the most telling response is to item five in the "Rules" box, see table 2.40: only 12.2 percent of the students felt that the rules were both

Table 2.40.   Truancy Rules as Understood by Students

1. My School Has Strict Rules:
   Agree = 43.4%   Disagree = 37.1%   Don't Know = 19.5%

2. Cutting Gets You into Trouble:
   Agree = 65.7%   Disagree = 21.7%   Don't Know =12.6%

3. School Has NO Real Written Rules:
   Agree = 63.0%   Disagree = 22.9%   Don't Know = 14.2%

4. Those Cutting Must Make Up Their Work:
   Agree = 41.6%   Disagree = 41.1   Don't Know = 17.3%

5. Rules Are Clear and Students Follow Them:
   Agree = 12.2%   Disagree = 66.4%   Don't Know = 22.4%

clear and followed. Similarly, item 3 found that 63 percent of the students believe that their schools have no written rules.

Correlation of "Rule Clarity" with Other Measures of Student Support

As shown in table 2.43, when we correlate these items as a sub-scale, My School's Rules, with the other subscales, Clear Rules related significantly to three areas: Teachers' Caring (Coefficient = .2430**), Parent Involvement and Help (.2181*), and School Organization and Quality (.4245**). Rules, then, seem most strongly correlated with students' overall perception of the school as orderly, safe, well-run, helpful, clean, and happy.

Thus, overall, students seem somewhat confused about their schools' rules on truancy. On some items, such as making up their work when absent, the sample students seem evenly divided at around 40 percent agreeing and 40 percent, disagreeing. Yet, in some ways, students believe that they get into trouble for cutting and skipping, even though rules are not explicit on this. We found about two-thirds of the students disagree with the statement that their "school rules are clear and students follow them." (See table 2.40.)

6. Truancy and Students' Feelings toward their School and Home

The last section of the analysis relates students' attitudes and feelings toward their school, teachers, parents, and selves and their level of truancy.

School Truancy and Students' Recommendation of School

In examining student satisfaction as indicated by their willingness to recommend their school to friends and frequency of cutting school "Often," we discovered that 23.3 percent of students who indicated that, they would not recommend cut "Often" by 27.3 percent. In comparison, those students who apparently were highly satisfied with their school and would recommend, cut at lower level: 11.1 percent. In fact, as the levels of satisfaction decline from "Yes," to "Somewhat," to "Don't Know," to "Maybe," to "No," the levels of cutting rise more or less in linear fashion: "Yes" at 11.1 percent cutting often, "Somewhat" at 17.7 percent,

Table 2.41.   School Truancy by Students' Willingness to Recommend Their School to Friends ("Satisfaction" Measure)

"I would recommend my school to a friend."

Truant from School	Yes, I Would	Somewhat	Don't Know	Maybe I Would	No, I Wouldn't	Total Responses
Truant School Often	1 (11.1%)	3 (17.7%)	3 (18.2%)	5 (31.3%)	9 (27.3%)	20 (23.3%)
Truant Sometimes	8 (88.9%)	14 (82.3%)	9 (81.8%)	11 (68.8%)	24 (72.7%)	66 (76.7%)
Total Truant	9 (36.0%)	17 (34.0%)	11 (31.4%)	16 (48.9%)	33 (54.1%)	86 (39.1%)
Never Truant	1 (64.0%)	33 (66.0%)	24 (68.6%)	33 (45.9%)	28 (45.9%)	134 (60.9%)
Total Sample	25 (100%)	50 (100%)	35 (100%)	49 (100%)	61 (100%)	220 (100%)

"Don't Know" at 18.2 percent, and "Maybe" recommend at 31.3 percent, for overall average of cutting "Often" at 23.3 percent.

Furthermore, the data on student satisfaction and "Never" cutting show a similar relationship. That, as the level of satisfaction goes down (as indicted by whether the standard recommends the school or not), as the Never Cuts also goes down, meaning that truancy is rising Data indicate (for example, that for the "Yes, I would recommend," their Never Cutting is high at 64.0 percent). For those more dissatisfied, saying "Maybe" I'd recommend or "No" I would not, the "Never" cutting has dipped to 45.9 percent and 45.9 percent, meaning that school truancy behavior is increasing. Hence, satisfaction with school may be a powerful predictor of whether pupils attend or not. However, the differences in truancy by students' recommending the school to a friend were not significant, as measured by a Chi Square test: 17.64, d.f. = 12, $p < .127$

Student Attitudes: Toward School, Teachers, Home, and Self to Cutting School and Class

The concept behind this exercise is that truancy is an action taken as the result of a complex process. Influencing this process are the feelings and beliefs of students about the following:

a. My Academic Progress

Students may be truant at a higher rate if they are dissatisfied with the education they are receiving. Stoll and O'Keeffe's data in England (1989) point to the relationship between truancy and the quality of learning in the students' schools.

Thus, the *Student Truancy and Attendance Review* (STAR) instrument asks students whether they "Agree Strong" = 5, "Agree Somewhat" = 4, "Neither Agree Nor Disagree" = 3, "Disagree Somewhat" = 2, and "Disagree Strongly" = 1 with statements such as: "I really learn by subjects and lessons in class." "I make good grades in most of my courses." These elicit information on students' perceptions of their own academic standing and progress—as a possible predictor of attending classes and school or not.

b. My Teachers

Critical to all education is the teacher. Thus, good teachers, respected and beloved by their students, are less likely to have truancy in their classrooms. Caring teachers are powerful incentives to attend—and a critical disincentive to cut. STAR's statements include: "My teachers really care about me as a person." "My teachers keep their classes interesting and exciting."

c. My Friends

Since we know that students are truant with friends, perhaps they are also attending with friends as well. Thus, students who perceive themselves as having caring, supportive colleagues at school may attend with greater frequency. The STAR's statements include such items as: "I have a good group of friends in my school who help me." My friends miss me and care about me when I'm not at school."

d. My Parents/Guardian's Help

Besides school support, the home is also an important influence on students' attending school. Ziesemer (1984) argues persuasively that it is too easy to blame the family for the child's truancy; nevertheless, some contend that in combination with weak affiliations at school, students may be likely to miss school. Thus, the STAR instrument examines the role of parents and guardians in promoting school and class attendance and school goals and purposes. Items include: "My parent(s)/guardian(s) really care that I do well in school." "My parents talk to my teachers about my work."

e. About My School

Students are more likely to attend a school that is supportive, safe, nice, and well-run. Thus, STAR asks students to react to such items as: "My school is a safe, nice place to go." "My school is well run." "Everyone helps everybody in my school."

f. Extra-Curricular/Co-Curricular Involvement

Another theory of why students attend school is their interest in sports, clubs, and other co-curricular activities. Participation has several obvious values: it engages students in visible activities at school; and it also puts students in close contact with other students and faculty (club sponsors and athletic coaches) who can help students to attend and do well at school. STAR includes: "I am involved in sports or other activities (clubs) at my school." "I like joining activities so I can spend more time with my friends."

g. Feeling Good about Myself

The last section of STAR examines the self-concept of students, which may be the net effect of the other dimensions of the instrument. Thus, students who have caring teachers, in a well-run, safe, and happy school, with an engaging co-curricula, with parents who help and care, and who are doing well academically may make the calculation that going to school is not all that bad. Involvement and engagement may then lead to a strong sense of self-worth and self-esteem, which may promote school attendance in the rational processes of determining whether to cut or go. Items in STAR include: "I really feel good about myself." "I am unhappy at school because I'm not getting anywhere."

Reliability

The reliability of these eight measures was determined by computing a coefficient Alpha for each sub-scale cluster of items. Table 2.42 shows the sub-scales, the number of items in each, the adjusted mean (standardized

Table 2.42.   Reliability Measures for Eight STAR Sub-Scales

	I. Items by Sub-Scale	II. Full/ Adj. Mean	III. Standard Deviation*	IV. Alpha	V. Standard Item Alpha
1. Academic Progress: Adjust Mean	5	19.1875* 3.84	3.6527**	.6729	.6905
2. Teacher Caring	4	13.5069 3.38	4.3485	.8242	.8257
3. Friends Support	6	20.1458 3.36	5.5596	.7439	.7484
4. Parent Support	7	22.2639 3.18	6.4753	.7587	.7614
5. School Climate	5	13.1181 2.62	5.3159	.8449	.8443
6. Extra-Curricular Involvement	5	14.8819 2.98	5.0084	.6464	.6503
7. Self-Concept	6	21.9583 3.66	3.9417	.4584	.4857
8. Rule Clarity	5	15.5833 3.12	4.34.28	.5545	.5639

*Adjusted Mean: full mean is divided by the number of sub-scale items, reducing the differences based on the number of items per sub-scale to a score of between 5 = Agree Strongly to 1 = Disagree Strongly, as presented in the STAR Likert scale.
** The Standard Deviation is based on the full-score, not the adjusted score, as shown in column 2, top line of each cell.

for the number of items to reduce it to between 1 and 5), the standard deviation, and the Alpha and Standardized Item Alpha of reliability. As displayed in column IV, the Alpha coefficients indicate from high to moderate levels of reliability, with "Teacher Caring" at .8242, "Friends Support" at .7439, "Parent Support" showing .7587, and "School Climate" was .8449. At the lower end, we still find fairly strong reliability measure (.7000 and above is considered highly reliable) with "Academic Progress" at .6729 and students' "Self-Concept" with .4584.

Examining the Relationship between Students' Attitudes and Truancy Behaviors, Satisfaction, and Academic Progress

Correlation Analysis

As shown in table 2.43, student truancy behaviors (being absent from both class and school) are negatively and often significantly correlated

Table 2.43.   Correlation of Cutting School and Class with Student Attitudes

	Cutting Class	Cutting School	Academic Progress	Teacher Caring	Friends Caring	Parental Support	School Climate	Extra-Curricular Activities	Self-Concept	School Rules
Cutting Class	1.000									
Cutting School	-.379**	1.000								
Academic Progress	-.186*	-.224*	1.000							
Teacher Caring	-.306**	-.222*	.356**	1.000						
Friends Caring	-.155	-.140	.241**	.404**	1.000					
Parental Support	-.316**	-.293**	.194**	.393**	.320**	1.000				
School Climate	-.016	-.196*	.067	.412**	.322**	.258	1.000			
Extra-Curricular Activities	.132	-.121	.085	.284**	.272**	.223**	.343**	1.000		
Self-Concept	-.227**	-.288**	.035	.182*	.223**	.231**	.095	.096	1.000	
School Rules	-.138	-.200	.035	.211*	.172*	.255**	.4174**	.179*	.060	1.000

1-tail Significance: * = .01   ** = .001

with certain key student feelings and attitudes. For example, as indicated in column 1, "Teacher Caring" (–.3055), "Parental Support" (–.3160), and student "Self-Concept" (–.2268) are significant at the .001 level, meaning that the stronger these perceptions of students' school environment, the less likely students are to play hooky. Even "Academic Progress" (–.1856) is correlated negatively at the .01 level.

Similarly, cutting school correlates negatively with "Parental Support" (–.2934) and "Self-Concept" (–.2882) at the p = .001 level of signifi- cance, while "Teacher Caring" (–.2217), "Academic Progress" (–.2240), "School Climate" (–.1955), and "School Rules" (–.1995) are negatively related at the p = .01 level of significance. Note that the variable "School Rules" is significant for "Cutting School" but not for "Cutting Class," in- dicating a bit more slippage in rule-clarity and enforcement once students are in the building. Thus, students can get away with truancy by talking themselves out of attending a particular class ("I'm sick," "I'm having my period," "I've got to call my allergist"), which hardly works when staying home and then having to report the absence (bring a note from home) the next day.

Correlation of Academic Progress and Other Attitudes

Correlation analyses were also performed on the relationship be- tween these students' attitudes and their sense of "Academic Progress." Table 2.43, column 3, shows that academic progress correlates posi- tively and significantly with "Teacher Caring" (.3557) and "Friends Caring" (.2406). As displayed in table 2.42, column 4, the Alpha coef- ficients indicate from high to moderate levels of reliability, with "Teacher Caring" at .8242, "Friends Support" at .7439, "Parent Sup- port" showing .7587, and "School Climate" was .8449. At the lower end, we still find fairly strong reliability measure (.7000 and above is considered highly reliable) with "Academic Progress" at .6729, stu- dents' "Self-Concept" with .4584. strong Self-Concept (.4161), signif- icant at the .001 level. "Parental Support" (.1937) was significant at the .01 level.

Of all the variables in this study, the three that seemed to correlate with other variables most consistently were "Teacher Caring," "Friends Caring," and "Parental Support." Thus, as these data show, caring teachers, supportive friends, and high self-esteem correlate significantly and positively with a sense of making academic progress in school, and negatively relate to cutting school and classes.

Multiple Regression Analysis

We then tested the unique and combined contribution of the student attitudes, demographic variables, and school contextual variables to four dependent variables: (a) the level of *School Truancy* ('blanket" truancy); (b) *Classroom Truancy* ("post-registration") for students already at school; (c) *Students' Recommending their School to a Friend*—a measure of students' satisfaction and pride in their school; and (d) *Students' Academic Progress* as self-reported by respondents. We sought to perform a more fine-tuned analysis of the relationships between student, home, school and truancy, performance, and satisfaction; we hoped to see to what degree student characteristics and attitudes about their teachers, schools, home, and rules at school would predict their levels of truancy, happiness with their school, and sense of academic accomplishment.

1. Predicting Truancy

Table 2.44 shows the results when we regressed both blanket and post-registration truancy levels against the dimensions of student attitudes, school and student characteristics. For "Cutting School" (columns 1–3, table 2.44), a multiple R of .41 explained 17 percent of the variance, but only the sex of the student ($\beta = .17$, p < .03) and parental support ($\beta = -.22$, p < .01) had a significant and unique effect on school truancy. However, note that the student attitude variables ("Academic Grades," "Rule Clarity," "Parent Support," "Academic Progress," "School Site," and "Pupil's Age") were all inversely related to school truancy, while the demographic variables ("Grade Level," "Student Sex," and "Student Ethnicity") were positively related. Thus, the tendency in the data is for students who feel positive about their grades, the rules in their school, parent support, and their academic progress to have less cutting.

Similar findings were noted for "Cutting Class," as shown in table 2.44, columns 4–6. A multiple R of .47 ($p < .0001$) explained 23 percent of the variance in truancy. But unlike school truancy, class cutting behavior

Table 2.44. Multiple Regression Analysis of Truancy and Student Attitudes, Characteristics, and School Descriptors

	Truancy: Cutting School			Truancy: Cutting Classes		
	Beta*	T	p	Beta*	T	p
Academic Grades	−.13	−1.44	.15	−.19	−2.26	.03
Grade Level	.18	1.05	.29	.32	1.97	.05
Rule Clarity	−.12	−1.46	.15	−.11	−1.36	.17
Student Sex	.17	2.20	.03	.02	.331	.92
Student Ethnicity	.08	.98	.32	.32	.084	.04
Teacher Caring	.04	.46	.65	−.18	−2.08	.001
Parent Support	−.22	−2.66	.01	−.24	−2.86	.005
Academic Progress	−.08	−.90	.37	.09	1.01	.31
School Site	−.10	−.10	.32	.08	.80	.43
Pupil's Age	−.12	−.75	.45	−.17	−1.05	.30

$R = .41**$ $R = .47**$
$R^2 = .17**$
$R^2 = .23**$ Adjusted $R^2 = .11**$ Adjusted $R^2 = .18**$
$p = .0001$

seems more affected by a larger cluster of pupil attitudes and characteristics, including their "Academic Grades" ($\beta = -.19$, p < .03), "Grade Level" ($\beta = .32$, p = .05), "Ethnicity" ($\beta = .32$, p = .04), "Teacher Caring" ($\beta = -.18$, p = .001), and "Parental Support" ($\beta = -24$, p = .005).

The greater number of significant explanatory variables for classroom cutting over school truancy may result from the considerably higher level of skipping classes over cutting school; or perhaps the greater variation in post-registration truancy makes that cutting more sensitive to the interests and behaviors of teachers and parents, to the rules and atmosphere in the school, and to the ethnicity and grade level of students. Both equations, however, were significant at the .0001 level.

2. Students' Academic Progress and Satisfaction

Two additional multiple regression equations were used to see to what degree student attitudes affected their sense of "Academic Progress" and "Satisfaction with School," as measured by asking them to what degree they would recommend their school to a friend. Table 2.45 shows the results of the multiple regressions. In relating student satisfaction, measured by asking, "Would you recommend this school to a friend?", we were able

Table 2.45. Multiple Regression Analysis of Student Attitudes, Academic Progress, and Student Satisfaction "Would you recommend your school to a friend?"

Satisfaction with School	Academic Progress					
	Beta*	T	p	Beta*	T	p
Academic Grades	.07	.794	.43	.43	6.29	.001
Grade Level	.14	.89	.38	−.40	−2.75	.01
Rule Clarity	.06	.76	.45	−.03	−.34	−.73
Student Sex	.94	1.29	.20	.43	.64	.52
Student Ethnicity	−.09	−1.24	.22	−.16	−2.32	.02
Teacher Caring	.019	.22	.83	.22	2.80	.01
Parent Support	−.027	−.34	.74	.060	.80	.42
Academic Progress	−.04	−.51	.61	.02	.22	.82
School Site	.43	4.59	.00	.27	1.89	.06
Pupil's Age	−.32	−2.05	.04		2.62	.01

$R = .50$** $R = .60$**
$R^2 = .25$** $R^2 = .36$** Adjusted $R^2 = .20$**
Adjusted $R^2 = .33$** $p = .0001$

to produce another dependent variable, and to regress it against the student attitude and demographic variables, producing a multiple R of .50 that explains 25 percent of the variance. Of the ten variables, only "School Site" (.43, p < .001) and "Pupil's Age" (−.32, p < .04) had a significance impact on satisfaction among students.

However, the "Academic Progress" sub-scale of the STAR instrument gives some sense of whether students are doing well, at least in their own eyes. This well-being may be related to the environment and demographics of their schools. Table 2.45, columns 4-6, present the Betas for these independent variables. When regressed against "Academic Progress," the R is .60 and explains 33 percent of the variance. All were significant at the $p < .0001$. Thus, the regression seems to indicate that truancy is related to certain key personal and environmental variables, particularly attending school with caring teachers and supportive families. Cutting classes appears more sensitive to the setting and the conditions under which students attend their schools.

In summary, truancy is still a problem; in fact, it appears to be more widespread and acceptable than the literature predicted. Yet, this study shows that certain key variables may relate negatively to skipping out of school and classes. A caring, supportive teacher, parent, and friend appear to affect truancy negatively. School rules, although many students found them ambiguous if non-existent, may make the guidelines clearer and curtail some truant behavior. And a well-run, well-organized, pleasant school (school climate) may also bring down the truancy rate a bit.

The final chapter addresses the question: What can and should be done to lure students back to school, to reduce the skipping and cutting that seem too widespread? Again, we urge an avoidance of easy "causes" (e.g., the kids these days are no good, the problem is related to character flaws or personal weakness).

Instead, educators, policy-makers, parents, school board members, and concerned citizens should look the situation in the face: strong action is needed; schools need to "see" their students differently, as though they were "paying customers" that need to be listened to, heeded, and involved. Being conscripted to school, forced to sit through unwanted classes and experiences, and then told to enjoy it, seems a triple insult. It's not that the school should go soft; our data indicate that schools and districts have failed to make the rules clear, to engage the students in settings and supporting them, and then to stick by the joint pact, as discussed in the next chapter. Instead, much can be done to lower the rates of truancy and to engage students, teachers, parents, and community in the improvement of students' education.

3

Fighting Truancy: A Three-Pronged Approach

The concept that schools should not make children hate school appears to be quite reasonable.

—Travis, 1995, p. 434

During the past thirty years, educators in the United States have implemented costly reforms for all students aimed at reversing the pattern of school failure. These education problems often manifested themselves as school non-attendance, loss of academic focus and learning, poor grades, more truancy, and eventually drop-out and the narrowing of future economic opportunities. Although the nation has increased its pre-school programs, a host of bilingual initiatives, mainstreaming of challenged and handicapped pupils, and a restructuring agenda including the full-service school, the level of truancy remains a problem. And unfortunately, this study and other research indicate that missing school is more common than the literature predicted.

A review of the history of education in this country suggests that truancy is not a modern dilemma. The problem of early school leavers was a concern for school administrators in the nineteenth century. In fact, according to some statistics, only one-third of the students required to attend public school actually did so. In the early part of the twentieth century, more than two-thirds of all school absences were not related to illness.

Contemporary discourse on truancy—rooted in the rationale for compulsory schooling—is important not only because it allows us to trace the priorities and practices of public education, but also because it verifies that mandatory school attendance is fully engraved in the American consciousness and is almost unquestionable.

In a compelling paper, "Ways of Seeing: An Essay on the History of Compulsory Schooling," David Tyack (1976) presents basic data on changes in compulsory attendance legislature in the United States during the nineteenth and twentieth centuries. Tyack then describes at least five explanations that may account for the phenomenon of compulsory schooling. First, in the throws of nationalism, compulsory education was a convenient way of ensuring civic knowledge and participation. Second, as the United States became more culturally and ethnically diverse, "common school" attendance was one way of creating the new American character and a sense of unity.

Third, as the "one best system," to use Tyack's famous phrase, became larger and more bureaucratic, compulsory attendance laws provided an ever-rising number of students to the system. Fourth, according to Tyack, compulsory education served a key economic function: preparing workers to contribute their human capital to national expansion. Finally, from a Marxist perspective, compulsory education ensured that every student learned "how the system worked" from life inside schools, good preparation for assuming their station in the economic pecking order. Thus, Tyack's essay provides alternative "ways of seeing" compulsory school attendance and, by implication, some understanding of why most American students cut school during their education careers.

AN ALTERNATIVE WAY OF SEEING

This study treats truancy as a rational choice. As such, it shifts our focus from seeing a few truant students as troubled malcontents, to understanding truancy as a universal rational response. Our research shows that certain key variables relate negatively (inversely) to skipping school and classes, including the positive influence of caring, supportive teachers, parents, or friends. Although many students found school rules to be ambiguous, or non-existent, these strictures may be of some use in guiding students and reducing truant behavior. And an organized, well-run, and pleasant school with a positive school climate may also bring down the truancy rate a bit.

A few findings were unexpected. For example, student involvement in extra-curricular activities did have a negative (inverse) relationship to cutting but not a significant one. Perhaps our sample students were not heavily involved in these activities and thus were not benefiting themselves from playing a sport or joining a club. Further research on this topic is necessary. Caring friends, likewise, was negatively related to truancy but again, not significantly—although it was significantly and positively related to academic progress. Perhaps, friends can be a temptation to go AWOL since most students reported that they were truant with their buddies.

A TIME TO ACT

Reducing truancy in American schools should be a top priority. As research shows, missing class hampers both learning and achievement. And since the practice of unacceptable absences is increasing, with over two-thirds of our sample and the British pupils cutting class, we need to consider actions to reduce and eliminate students' missing their education at school. Experts in reducing truancy are of three minds.

Society's Problems Are Schools' Problems

The first group of researchers and practitioners—well represented in the literature and in the field—see skipping school and classes as both an indicator and a result of wider societal problems. As such, teachers and other educators are virtually helpless in empowering students to overcome their social and economic problems outside of school. This approach has its roots in the minds of those who see some students as "at-risk," "deficient," and "disadvantaged." Gary Natriello explains:

> Conditions outside the school may fail to provide support for students to attend regularly and continue in school. Conditions that contribute to truancy and early school leaving include a variety of personal, familial, and community problems such as teenage pregnancy, alcohol and drug abuse, delinquent gang membership, family violence and child abuse, family social and financial needs requiring students to be at home or to find work, and social

disorganized communities with high rates of crime. (1994, p. 1603; see also Natriello et al., 1990)

Experts on truancy in this camp have little of practical use to recommend since the problems are so enormous and are mostly found beyond the walls of the schools. Until the society eliminates poverty, racism, sexism, crime, teenage pregnancy, and other debilitating conditions, this group believes, it will be difficult to reduce the truancy rates. For, after all, students are subject to the pressures and problems around them.

The best that these social critics can do is to suggest making school programs more relevant to children "at risk." In part, this means helping schools to bridge the gap between the culture of the school and the community. Making the school's curricula more multicultural, relevant, and practical seems appropriate for those viewing the problem as essentially contextual. For example, Natriello suggests that "strategies designed to address unsupportive outside conditions have involved the development of new relationships between families and schools, and the integration of education and human services to address the social and economic problems that impede progress through school" (1994, p. 1606).

Even though this socio-environmental approach is useful in alerting educators to the needs of their students, it falls short of coping directly and immediately with the problems of cutting and skipping. Something more is required.

Getting Tough with Truants

A second school of thought treats the problem head-on. Since being absent for no legitimate reason is illegal in most states and school districts, education authorities—working closely with the police, human services, and juvenile authorities—can and do take stronger action. As Dr. Kara Gae Wilson, superintendent of schools of Tulsa County, Oklahoma, argues, districts have a whole repertoire of steps to cope with truancy, "*but no method has been as effective as taking truants to court*" (Wilson, 1993, p. 43; emphases added).

Even though local district attorneys have long had the right to prosecute the parents and guardians of truants, Dr. Wilson found that few such legal actions were taken—until, that is, the late 1980s when she took over as

Tulsa County superintendent. She writes in the *American School Board Journal*:

> What happens when a student and family are taken to court for truancy violation? In the first three years of Tulsa County's crackdown on truancy, we filed more than 600 cases, resulting in a 45 percent reduction in the dropout rate. In a large majority of cases, the defendant either pled guilty and paid the required fine or the case was dismissed because parents agreed to place their children in alternative programs or different school districts. The most common outcomes of the 648 cases filed between 1989 and 1992 were as follows:
>
> - Pled guilty: 230;
> - Case dismissed: 221;
> - Case stricken because parents or guardian could not be found: 91;
> - Bench warrants issued: 47;
> - Trials: 14 guilty; and
> - 4 not guilty." (Wilson, 1993, p. 43)

For those taking this law-and-order approach, Dr. Wilson suggests that school administrators do the following: (a) Check state laws to see if fines can be imposed on the family for student truancy; (b) Convince the local district attorney to prosecute truant families; (c) Build a uniform reporting system in all schools for detecting students who are truant; (d) Appoint an attendance officer in each district to handle cases; (e) Prosecute cases of truancy in district, not juvenile courts; (f) Work with a judge who shares an interest in prosecuting truancy; (g) Offer help and training for parents brought into court; and (h) Inform the news media of your actions to keep public pressure focused on the anti-truancy effort.

While Wilson recognizes that prosecuting truancy under law is a national "shame," she asserts that without strict laws and active enforcement, many students will not take these requirements seriously and attendance will drop. However, this "get tough" method treats the symptoms of truancy, not the causes. It may be hard to sustain this legal effort without looking beyond the skipping to the reasons that students go truant.

Furthermore, our research shows that most of the illegal absenteeism is *not* from cutting school (students are checked "present" on the morning roll call); instead, students are skipping class *after they get to school*. Such "post-registration truancy," to use the British term, is more difficult to prosecute in court since parents are not usually to blame. Families, after all, did their part by seeing that their children arrived at school safe, sound, and on time. It's the school-site authorities who somehow let students malinger in the corridors, congregate behind the gym, move off campus to the local student hangouts, or simply go their own way.

Our survey indicated that many students left the school grounds and made their way home. Students recorded on the STAR survey that when they skipped class, they congregated on the playground, they walked home, went to "a homeboy's house," "hang outside," "a friend's house," "everywhere," "mama's house," "none of your business," "wherever I want to," "out to eat, halls, anywhere," and "to work." An account from one of New York City's leading schools tells how an elite magnet school suffers truancy during the day: students simply sit in the cafeteria instead of attending classes—and no one seems to care.

So, instead of superintendents, truant officers, and district attorneys dragging the family into court for negligence, "contributing to the delinquency of minors," or violating the state's compulsory attendance laws, the shoe may belong on the other foot. Parents and guardians might have grounds for a malpractice suit against the schools for letting their children wander around campus unnoticed, leave the school grounds without supervision during times when parents assume that the adults at school are in charge, or for tacitly condoning illegal behavior by not notifying the home every time a student "goes missing" during the day. What would happen if a student were to leave school illegally during regular class hours and, Heaven forbid, were injured or killed (at a time when the family assumes that the school is responsible)?

Thus, the "take-them-to-court" approach has some great advantages and difficulties. It is pro-active. Clearly, it signals to the community that truancy is unacceptable and that the authorities are doing what they can to stop this practice. But this method has problems as well. First, it puts the school into the police and prosecution business; second, it is mainly limited to students' missing school, not just classes while at school. Our data show that class skipping is more common than missing a whole day of school. And third, it may be difficult to maintain a program such as Tulsa's, as Dr. Wilson admits.

Treat Students as Education's Consumers and Clients

A third method, done perhaps in combination with the previous two approaches, may hold great promise. In addition to understanding the needs and problems of students today (method one) and to using the full force of the law where necessary (method two), school leaders should also consider treating students as their clients, their consumers, and moving to engage students in the process of their own education.

A FEW USEFUL RECOMMENDATIONS

Since truancy is a complex, many-sided concern, the recommendations are directed to administrators, teachers, parents, students, and others concerned about getting students to attend school regularly. Ten bits of advice might be useful in tackling the problems of truancy of all sorts in schools.

1. *Listen to the Students:* Seeking to understand students' points of view and valuing their perspectives are essential to creating meaningful school communities. Alienation and disengagement from learning are all too common experiences for students. As Hickerson (1966) explains: "Children abandon school in the second grade attitudinally, and in the tenth physically, not because they are 'stupid' but because they don't care. They have been estranged from school" (Hickerson, 1966, p. 42).

Often, we act as though students are the products or conscripts of school, when, in fact students must be seen as consumers who make choices about what they will learn and when. If classes are oppressive, dull, and unchallenging, students are provoked to cry out and complain. They may passively resist in class or students may choose not to attend certain classes at all, a variation on the "exit, voice, and loyalty" theme advanced by Hirschman (1970).

The authors of *The Shopping Mall High School* (Powell, Farrar and Cohen, 1985) found that consumerism was the dominant motif of education in the United States. Powell and colleagues wrote, "The centrality of variety, choice, neutrality in the mall is not seen by insiders as a cop-out, a conspiracy to expect the least. They regard these features, instead, as enabling high schools to meet as many adolescents' needs as possible"

(p. 61). Unfortunately, students are not usually asked about the "products" in the mall, as the metaphor implies, nor are their concerns and needs being considered when designing the courses and activities. Powell and associates continue: "Few characteristics of the shopping mall high school are more significant than the existence of unspecial students in the middle who are ignored and poorly served" (p. 173). Too often, the unspecial and the unspoken are neglected and left alone. Who would blame these young people for being truant?

Our study is especially interested in the students' perspectives. Through focused interviews, we wanted to hear the authentic voices of students talking about their school experiences. Some talked about getting lost in schools that are too large and impersonal. One boy painfully concluded, "No one knows I'm there. So what's the difference?" A reflective student commented, "I don't think I'm ready for high school. I was happier in junior high. I did better."

In talking about their teachers, the students readily identified the best teachers as those who cared about them in and out of classes. Caring meant helping them when the work was difficult. One student remarked, "I know Ms. Miller wants me to do well. She told me so." Another commented, "She doesn't think you're stupid. She likes when you ask questions."

Many of the students complained about boring classes. "We just sit there," echoed one student. "I don't like doing the same thing every day. It gets boring," complained another. One student remembered working together with other students on a project: "That was fun. It was different." Frankly, the students' comments were not surprising but confirming of Sarason's (1983) indictment that schools generally are and have been uninteresting places for students and others. Classrooms are intellectually boring places. According to Sarason (1983), developments in the mass media have created for young people an unbridgeable gulf between the classroom and the real world.

Noting that dropouts have repeatedly cited boredom as a major reason for leaving school, the influence of the curriculum is critical in affecting student success and failure (Fine, 1991). From the students' perspective the choice of curriculum often seems arbitrary. Frequently, students were puzzled by grouping practices in schools and the restriction on certain courses they were then allowed to take. One student said, "I wanted to take biology but everyone in my group was scheduled for physical science. I really didn't like that."

If students do not have the opportunity to pursue their interests, they should at least be offered subjects that are meaningful to their personal dreams. Learning is enhanced when the curriculum engages the cognitive, social, and affective needs and interests of students. In discussing the importance of seeking to uncover the student's perceptions and interests, John Dewey wrote: "Selected, utilized, emphasized, [activities of interest to students] may mark a turning point for good in the child's whole career; neglected, an opportunity goes, never to be recalled (1902, p. 14). Listening to students is a starting point as teachers and administrators seek to re-create meaningful school experiences that students will choose.

2. Treat Truancy as a Universal Behavior: Educators need to stop applying a "deficit" model to students who cut. Children of every conceivable background make daily choices that can alter their life's course. We need to see everyone as a potential truant: boys and girls, Anglos and Latinos, African Americans and Asian Americans, poor and middle class. This research shows the near universality of truancy, a condition brought on by experience in the system and a "learning curve" of how to cut and skip with impunity. Rules are not always clear. Catching students rarely happens—particularly within the building. And contact with the home and punishment for missing their education seem spotty at best. Thus, we need a new viewpoint and new action.

The challenge is to reconceptualize the role of the school and the relationship between the school, the community, and society. A number of imaginative initiatives have been developed in Britain to address the particular needs of habitual truants. In the United States, Cities in Schools (CIS), a national charitable organization, is working in partnership with business, community, social, and welfare agencies to combat truancy and drop-out. CIS brings together a team of professionals to work in the schools with children to enhance their self-esteem and to provide personal and educational skills that kids need to stay in school. In this country, also, full-service schools offer a range of social agencies with a wide spectrum of essential services to help all children—but particularly those at risk. These child-centered plans build collaboration between various agencies in the name of the client: the child.

3. *Define and Differentiate the Types of Truancy:* This research and similar studies in English schools show that many more students cut class than skip school. Yet, state and local education agencies typically record only "blanket" or complete school absences and less often consider the high number of students who come to school, get "checked present," and then "book it," leaving the scene for playgrounds, back hallways, behind the gym, or the nearby soda shop. Until "post-registration" truancy is taken seriously, recorded, reported, and analyzed, educators, parents and other interested parties will continue to fool themselves about the nature and extent of the problem.

Paterson's (1989) distinction between the "endangered" and the "fearful" truant proves useful in understanding types of truants. We can find the concept of the "fearful truant" in the writings and observations of child guidance professionals in the 1930s and 1940s. The fearful truant or school phobic wishes to go to school but is afraid and remains at home. A more common theme in the literature, however, is the "endangered truant." This student is absent from school and/or class deliberately, may leave the building or remain on school grounds, and may cut alone or with others.

While some suggest a relationship between this truancy and delinquent behavior, a causal link has yet to be established. However, we do know that missing school and cutting a class are quite different transgressions. Since they may be brought on for different reasons, they should be recorded separately, managed differently, and treated as related but different conditions.

4. *Concentrate on Reducing Class Cutting:* By now, it is obvious that more effort should be devoted to attacking selective cutting. How many students arrive at schools only to cut classes all day? How many cut the same periods, courses, or teachers regularly? What analysis is made of these class-cutting behaviors? Is there adequate supervision of corridors, bathrooms, lunchrooms, playgrounds and other potential "hiding places"? Using the "choice theory" approach, administrators, teachers, and students need to discuss and act on class cutting, if it is a problem in their schools.

Thus, acting against traditional "truancy"—with the appropriate truant officers—has been almost exclusively for those kids not showing up at school: those on the "Absence List" excessively and for unexcused reasons. What about the students who slip away during school (and who are already marked "Present" for the day). Our data, like those in England from Stoll and O'Keeffe (1989), show that many more students cut classes than stay home: 68 percent compared to 38 percent. Perhaps, schools are less aware of what is going on under their noses.

Greater effort should be made to get students into class and out of halls and stairwells and to see that good data are available *period by period* on where students are. With new electronic means, students should be checked into classes every period. And for those at school but not in their classes, teachers should be alerted and discussions and other actions should be taken.

5. *Make School and District Truancy Policies and Rules Clearer:* We have some evidence that students are less likely to be truant if the school's rules are clearly explained and consistently and fairly enforced. A district-wide handbook on truancy and absences should be written, shared, approved, and applied. Parents and students should sign a notice that they know these policies and are prepared to support them. Supervision, notification, and punishment should be appropriate and well-publicized. Teachers who have a cutting problem should be helped. And periodic reviews and updating should be done to help improve these policies and practices. Goals should be set: for example, to reduce cutting and skipping by 10 percent per year in those schools with serious problems.

6. *Seek Teacher Support as the First Line of Defense:* Teachers have a major share of enforcing and influencing the truancy policies and practices in their schools. Several ways emerge: First, keeping their classroom alive, exciting, and engaging may help draw students to class and school. Second, teachers should be keenly aware of who's missing class by asking a simple question: "Has anyone seen Cathy or Keith today?"

"Yes, Mr./Ms Harkness, s/he was on the playground last period break and in the third period class," responds a student. Now what? Should the teacher go out to the playground? Contact the office? Send another student? And if the student appears the next day, what can be done?

The teacher is in the middle: this issue of teacher response, and the school backup for the teacher, are both critical to handling the cutting problem before too many days are lost. And what about the student who just misses school altogether? Perhaps a telephone call, which many schools make routinely? Perhaps a nice discussion with the student, not in an accusing way, but to find out what's happening: sickness, an infirm parent or grandparent, a bully who's after another student who cuts to save a beating?

These data, then, indicate the importance of caring, involved teachers in the control of truancy, both blanket and post-registration. Our correlation indicates that lower rates of cutting class are more highly (negatively) correlated with caring teachers. This difference may indicate that students cut and attend based on the teachers' expectations, demands, concerns, and excitement. Teachers, therefore, need to be closely involved with the truancy levels, and to feel that they can report students and will be heard.

7. *Engage Students in the Anti-Truancy Efforts:* Measures should be taken to discuss classes and courses with students: What can I do to make my algebra class more interesting to you? What bores you? Are you tired of spending the first fifteen minutes going over last night's homework or reviewing the test? Perhaps we should introduce something new and exciting at the beginning of each class, and then do the reviewing toward the end for those who need it—while the others move ahead. This discussion is best done by teachers, with their own students, to make it as non-threatening and productive as possible.

We have also seen successful "peer facilitator" programs at work in high schools since the early 1960s. Since the 1980s, students have been trained to listen and help other students with their problems in elementary and middle schools. In one study, "The Effects of a Peer Facilitator Intervention on Middle School Problem-Behavior Students," Tobias (1993) found evidence that middle school peer facilitators, especially eighth graders, can be particularly effective in improving pupil attitudes toward school and assisting to alleviate the problem of absenteeism. Both peer facilitators and the students with whom they worked benefited, as explained in this study.

8. *Help Parents to Share the Burden:* Truancy is a family problem, not just a concern of schools. Besides missing school, students who "hang out" on streets or in unsupervised homes, are apt to get into trouble. Parents have a right to know where their children are and to be assured that they are notified if their offspring are "somewhere else," as yet undetermined. A joint home-school effort around class-cutting and school-skipping is important if the problem is to be addressed.

As one newspaper account exclaimed: "Americans are growing tired of seeing gangs of teenagers hanging out during the day at shopping malls and in video arcades. People are worried about the rise of crime and the decline in schools standards, and are more demanding that parents take more responsibility for their children" (Wilce, 1993, p. 14).

9. *Treat Truancy as a Barometer of School Involvement:* For policy-makers and top administrators, truancy should be revisited and reconceived:

- Gather better information: track students who skip and cut.
- Alert school-site leadership to their standing on truancy on a weekly basis.
- Set out clear, district-wide goals and procedures for handling truancy: release them to parents, students, and educators in the schools.
- See cutting class as a more serious problem than skipping school. Take measures to handle these problems.

10. *Make the Reduction of Truancy a District and School Purpose and Process:* Finally, truancy data—of all kinds—should be gathered daily and analyzed weekly to see what the rates are by school and teacher. New policies, whatever they are, should be evaluated and reevaluated to see if they are working. When districts issue report cards on their individual school's achievements and problems, truancy (both from school and class) should be prominent. Schools that have nagging, persistent problems should be assessed and strong measures taken: meeting with parents and students, administrators and teachers. Careful attention should be given to reviewing the curricula and programs.

Finally, truancy may point to fundamental problems with the curriculum and program in schools. Are students bored? Is the work unchallenging, repetitive, and dull? Or is it too difficult? The work in England seems relevant here as well. As Stoll and O'Keeffe (1989, pp. 25–26) explain,

> Is the curriculum too easy and undemanding, or is it an unattainable "academic" abstraction for many pupils? The literature on the truancy problem has little to say on the subject. Eaton and Houghton found that "absence from school does appear to link with the adolescents' level of satisfaction there." Reid (1984) found his persistent absentees to be "generally unenthusiastic" about most subjects of the school curriculum in which they could perceive little purpose. Mitchell and Shepard (1987) found indications that many pupils had found their last year at school irrelevant to the world of work which they were about to enter. (pp. 25–26)

Another Englishman, A. S. Neill (1960), headmaster of the famous, libertarian Summerhill School, put it more bluntly. When asked by a parent for advice on the truancy of her son, Neill responded: "Speaking broadly, truancy means that the school is not good enough. If possible, try to send your boy to a school in which there is more freedom, more creativity, more love" (1960, p. 33).

Whatever the causes, whatever the costs, and whatever the techniques for coping with the problem, truancy remains a serious condition that affects our students, teachers, and the long-term needs of society. It deserves greater attention if our students are to have an opportunity to learn and achieve, and if our schools are to continue to carry out their responsibilities to children, home, and society.

Appendix:
Student Truancy and
Attendance Review (STAR-11)
(USA—May 1995)

Please fill in the items below. Do not put your name on this questionnaire. The results are strictly confidential and will not be shared with anyone. Thank you. Copyrighted, NYC., 1995

I. Demographics

1. Your grade level is: (check one)?
   ___8th grade ___9th ___10th ___11th ___12th ___Other

2. I am? (1) ___Male (2) ___Female

3. How old are you _____ years (age)?

4. I am: (1) ___African American (2) ___Latino(a)
   (3) ___Anglo-English (4) ___Asian (5) ___Other

5. My family speaks English at home:
   (3) ___Yes (2) ___Sometimes (1) ___No

6. About how long have you lived at your present address (home)?
   ____ years?

7. How long have you gone to this school?
   ___1st year ___2nd ___3rd ___4th ___More

8. Do you have a job after school? (1) ___Yes, regular (hours/week____)
   (2) ___Yes, sometimes (3) ___No

9. Do you have family responsibilities that might make you late or absent from school?
   (3) ___Yes, regularly (2) ___Yes, sometimes (1) ___No, not at all

10. Do you cut on a regular seasonal, monthly or weekly basis?
    (3) ___Yes, often (2) ___Sometimes (1) ___No, not at all

11. Overall, my grades are? (check one space please):
    (4) ___Excellent (A/B+) (3) ___Good (B/C+)
    (2) ___Fair(C/C–) (1) ___Failing

12. Would you recommend this school to your friends?
    (5) ___Yes, fully (4) ___Yes, somewhat (3) ___Don't know
    (2) ___Maybe (1) ___Rarely

13. Do you over-sleep, missing some school/classes?
    (3) ___Regularly (2) ___Sometimes (1) ___Rarely

II. Cutting or Skipping CLASS

14. In the last few years, have you cut class?
    (2) ___Often (1) ___Sometimes (0) ___Never

15. If *Often* or *Sometimes*, have you been caught?
    (0) ___Not CUT (1) ___Yes, cut and caught once
    (2) ___Yes, caught more than once (3) ___Cut, but *never* caught

16. If you cut class, did the school tell your parent(s)? (check one)
    (0) ___I did NOT cut (1) ___Yes, I cut and school told my
    parents/guardian (2) ___I cut, but the school never told my home

17. If you cut class, I cut:
    (1) ___Alone (2) ___With friends (3) ___Did *not* cut class at all

18. If you cut class, did you stay in the building? (select one):
    (1) ___Yes, sometimes (2) ___Yes, always (3) ___No, left
    (4) ___I did not cut. If you left school, where did you go? _____

19. If you cut class and were caught, were you punished?
    (1) ___I did not cut (2) ___Cut but was not punished
    (3) ___I was caught and punished. How?_____

20. Have you cut class by pretending, for example, to need a nurse, counsellor, or to find a lost item? (1) ___Yes (0) ___No
    Other tricks: What_____

III. Skipping (Cutting) SCHOOL

21. In the last year, have you cut school (check one?)
    (3) ___Often (2) ___Sometimes (3) ___Never

22. If *Often* or *Sometimes*, have you been caught?
    (0) ___I did not cut (skip) (1) ___Yes, I was caught several times
    (2) ___Yes, once (3)___I skip but I was never caught

23. If you cut school, did the school tell your parent(s)?
    (0) ___Not apply (1) ___Yes (2) ___No

24. If you cut school, I cut:
    (1) ___Alone (2) ___With friends (3) ___Do not cut school

25. If you cut school, and were caught, were you punished
    (0) ___Did not cut (1) ___Was not punished (3) ___I was punished
    How?_____

IV. Feelings Toward My School

Circle one number, with a:
5 = means "AGREE Strongly"   4 = "AGREE Somewhat"
3 = "Neither Agree nor Disagree"   2 = "DISAGREE Somewhat"
1 = "DISAGREE Strongly"

A. My Academic Progress

	Agree				Disagree
26. I really learn my subjects and lessons in class	5	4	3	2	1
27. I make good grades in most of my courses	5	4	3	2	1
28. I keep up and understand what's going on in my classes	5	4	3	2	1

29. The assignment (homework) is clear and I do it most of the time   **5 4 3 2 1**

30. I feel that my classes are too hard and I often can't keep up   **5 4 3 2 1**

B. My TEACHERS

	Agree		**Disagree**
31. My teachers really care about me as a person	**5 4 3 2 1**		
32. My teachers keep their classes interesting and exciting	**5 4 3 2 1**		
33. Teachers give me extra help if I fall behind	**5 4 3 2 1**		
34. The teachers really know their subjects and share their ideas	**5 4 3 2 1**		

C. My FRIENDS at School

	Agree		**Disagree**
35. Most of my friends do well in school	**5 4 3 2 1**		
36. I have a good group of friends in my school who help me	**5 4 3 2 1**		
37. I don't have many real friends at school	**5 4 3 2 1**		
38. My friends miss me and care when I'm not at school	**5 4 3 2 1**		
39. If I have problems, I have friends to share my feelings	**5 4 3 2 1**		
40. My friends encourage me to do well at school	**5 4 3 2 1**		

D. My Parent or Guardian's Help

	Agree		**Disagree**
41. My parent(s)/guardian(s) really care that I do well in school	**5 4 3 2 1**		
42. My parent(s)/guardian(s) know when I cut school or classes	**5 4 3 2 1**		

43. I can talk to a parent or guardian when I have
    problems   **5 4 3 2 1**

44. My parent(s)/guardian(s) help me with my
    homework   **5 4 3 2 1**

45. My parent(s)/guardian(s) are involved at my
    school   **5 4 3 2 1**

46. My parent(s)/guardian(s) ask me about my
    work at school   **5 4 3 2 1**

47. My parent(s)/guardian(s) talk to my teachers
    about my work   **5 4 3 2 1**

E. About My SCHOOL

         Agree   **Disagree**

48. My school is a safe, nice place to go   **5 4 3 2 1**
49. My school is well run   **5 4 3 2 1**
50. Everyone helps everybody in my school   **5 4 3 2 1**
51. The principal or some adult is really in charge   **5 4 3 2 1**
52. My school is clean and happy   **5 4 3 2 1**

F. Extra-Curricular Activities at School

         Agree   **Disagree**

53. I am involved in sports or other activities
    (clubs) at school   **5 4 3 2 1**

54. Most everyone supports the teams and
    activities at school   **5 4 3 2 1**

55. I don't participate in many extra-curricular
    activities   **5 4 3 2 1**

56. I like joining activities so I can spend more
    time with friends   **5 4 3 2 1**

57. School spirit is high about activities and
    everyone joins in   **5 4 3 2 1**

G. Feelings about Myself

		Agree				Disagree
58. I really feel good about myself		5	4	3	2	1
59. I feel that everyone puts me down in class		5	4	3	2	1
60. I feel good about myself because others look up to me		5	4	3	2	1
61. I feel good because school is happy place for me		5	4	3	2	1
62. I know that I will do well in life when I leave my school		5	4	3	2	1
63. I am unhappy at school because I'm not getting anywhere		5	4	3	2	1

V. My School's Rules

		Agree				Disagree
64. My school has strict rules about cutting classes		5	4	3	2	1
65. If you cut class, the rules say that you will get into trouble		5	4	3	2	1
66. My school has *no* real written rules or policies on cutting		5	4	3	2	1
67. If you cut class or school, you have to make up all the work		5	4	3	2	1
68. Rules are clear and students follow them		5	4	3	2	1

69. School #_____   70. School Type_____.

Dennis O'Keefe, Research Leader

References

Arnett, J. (1994). "Sensation seeking: A new conceptualization and a new scale," *Personality and Individual Differences*. Vol. 16, pp. 289–296.

Bayh, B. (1977). *Challenge for the Third Century: Education in a Safe Environment*. Washington, DC: U.S. Government Printing Office.

Birman, B. F. & G. Natriello (1978). "Perspectives on absenteeism in high schools." *Journal of Research and Development in Education*. 11:4, pp. 29–38.

Carnoy, M. & H. Levin (1976). *The Limits of School Reform*. New York: David McKay.

Coleman, James S. (1990). *Foundations of Social Theory*. Cambridge, MA: Belknap Press.

Dewey, J. (1902). *The Child and the Curriculum*. Chicago: University of Chicago Press.

Fine, M. (1991). *Framing Drop-outs on the Politics of an Urban Public High School*. Albany, NY: University of New York Press.

Finn, J. (1989). "Withdrawing from school," *Review of Educational Research, 59* (2), pp. 117–143.

Ghory, W. J., R. L. Sinclair & B. Robinson, (1988). "Considering marginal students," *Renewing School Curriculum*. In R. L. Sinclair and S. M. Nieta (eds.), *Renewing School Curriculum*. Boston: University of Massachusetts, Coalition for School Improvement.

Haller, E. J. (1992). "High school size and student indiscipline: Another aspect of the school consolidation issue," *Educational Evaluation and Policy Analysis*. 14:2, pp. 145–156.

Hickerson, N. (1966). *Education for Alienation*. Englewood Cliffs, NJ: Prentice-Hall.

Hirschman, A. O. (1970). *Exit, Voice and Loyalty.* Cambridge, MA: Harvard University Press.

Hofkins, D. (1994). "Radical declares war on alienation," *Times Educational Supplement.* July 22, 1994, No. 4073, p. 11.

Howard, R. C., J. P. Haynes & D. Atkinson, (1986, Summer). "Factors associated with juvenile detention and truancy," *Adolescence.* 21:82, pp. 357–364.

Jessor, R. & S. L. Jessor (1977). *Problem Behavior and Psychosocial Development: A Longitudinal Study of Youth.* New York: Academic Press.

Jones, C. (1996). "4 Students Shot Near a School in Brooklyn," *New York Times,* The Metropolitan Section, January 9, 1996, pp. B1, B4.

Kaeser, S. C. (1991). "Truancy." *Third International Encyclopedia of Education.* London: Pergamon Press, pp. 5299–5302.

Klein, R. (1994). "No skipping allowed," *Times Educational Supplement.* January 14, 1994, p. SS 20A.

Leithwood, K. & R. Aiken (1995). *Making Schools Smarter: A System for Monitoring School and District Progress.* Thousand Oaks, CA: Corwin Press.

Levine, R. (1984). "An assessment tool for early intervention in cases of truancy," *Social Work in Education,* Vol. 3, pp. 133–149.

Liu, X., H. B. Kaplan & W. Risser, (1992). "Decomposing the reciprocal relationship between academic achievement and general self-esteem," *Youth and Society.* 24:2, December 1992, pp. 123–148.

Mitchell, S. & M. Shepard (1980). *Reluctance to Go to School,* in L. Hersov & I. Berg, (eds.) *Out of School.* New York: John Wiley.

Moos, R. H. & B. S. Moos (1978). "Classroom social climate and student absences and grades," *Journal of Educational Psychology.* 70:2, pp. 263–269.

Murgatroyd, S. & C. Morgan (1992). *Total Quality Management and the School.* Philadelphia: Open University Press.

Natriello, G. (1994). "Dropouts, school leavers, and truancy." In *International Encyclopedia of Education.* 1st Edition. Vol. 3. London: Pergamon Press, pp. 1602–1607.

Natriello, G., E. McDill & A. Pallas (1990). *Schooling Disadvantaged Children: Racing against Catastrophe.* New York: Hart Publishing.

Neill, A. S. (1960). *Summerhill School: A New View of Childhood.* New York: St. Martin's Press.

Paterson, F. M. S. (1989). *Out of Place: Public Policy and the Emergence of Truancy.* London: Falmer Press.

Powell, A., E. Farrar & D. Cohen (1985). *The Shopping Mall High School.* Boston: Houghton-Mifflin.

Reid, K. (1985). *Truancy and School Absenteeism.* London: Hodder & Stoughton.

———. (1984). "Disruptive behavior and persistent school absenteeism," in N. Frude and H. Gault (eds.) *Disruptive Behavior in Schools.* New York: John Wiley.

Reynolds, D. R., S. St. L. Jones & S. Murgatroyd (1980). "School factors and truancy," in L. Hersov & I. Berg (eds.), *Out of School.* New York: John Wiley.

Reynolds, D. R. & S. Murgatroyd (1977). "The sociology of schooling and the absent pupil," in H. C. M. Carroll (ed.), *Absenteeism in South Wales.* Swansea: Faculty of Education.

Robins, L. N. & K. S. Ratcliff (1978). Long-Term Outcomes Associated with School Truancy. (Report No. UDO18069). Washington, DC: Public Health Services Department of Health, Education Welfare (ERIC Document Reproduction Service, No. ED 152893).

Rubin, J. C. (1994). "Gotham's new outrage: Truants!" *Time* (May 23, 1994), p. 22.

Sarason, S. (1983). *Schooling in America: Scapegoat or Salvation?* New York: Free Press.

Stallings, J., M. Needels & N. Staybrook (1979). *How to Change the Process of Testing Basic Reading Skills in Secondary Schools.* Menlo Park, CA: SRI International.

Stoll, P. & D. O'Keeffe (1989). *Officially Present: An Investigation into Post-Registration Truancy in Nine Maintained Schools.* London: The Education Unit, Institute of Economic Affairs.

Tobias, A. (1993, December). "The effects of a peer facilitator intervention on middle school problem-behavior students," *The Peer Facilitatory Quarterly.* Vol. 11, No. 2, pp. 45–51.

Travis, J. E. (1995). "Alienation from learning: School effects on students," *Journal of a Just and Caring Education.* 1:4 pp. 434–448.

Tyack, D. B. (1968). *The One Best System: History of Urban Education in America.* Cambridge, MA: Harvard University Press.

———. (1976). "Ways of Seeing: An Essay on the History of Compulsory Schooling." In *Complementary Methods for Research in Education.* R. M. Jaeger (ed.) Washington, D.C.: American Educational Research Association.

Wilce, H. (1993, June 3). "Mother in court over truant son," *Times Educational Supplement.* N.4066, p. 14.

Wilson, K. G. (1993). "Tough on truants: Take kids to court to keep in school," *The American School Board Journal.* April 1993, Board Briefings, pp. 43, 46.

Ziesemer, C. (1984). "Student and staff perception of truancy and court referrals," *Social Work in Education.* Vol. 3, pp. 167–177.

Zuckerman, M. (1984). "Sensation seeking: A comparative approach to a human trait," *Behavior and Brain Sciences.* Vol. 7, pp. 413–471.

Index

absence episodes, 10
acting out, 12
ADA. *See* average daily attendance
Aiken, R., 12
American School Board Journal, 77
anti-truancy efforts, 84
at-risk behavior, 10, 76
attendance director, 12
attendance officer, 77
average daily attendance (ADA),
9

Birman, B. F., 8
bounded rationality, 3
Bronx, New York, 27
Brooks, G., 1
bunking off. *See* post-registration

CIS. *See* Cities in Schools
Cities in Schools (CIS), 81
Cohen, D., 79
Coleman, James S., 14
compulsory attendance laws, 7–8
Crew, R., 10
cutting. *See* post-registration

deficit model, 10
Dewey, J., 81
discouraging attendance, 7

education: compulsory, 74; history of,
73; one best system of, 74; value
of, 8
engagement, 12
ethnicity and truancy, 10; by gender,
36–37; faking illnesses, 40; with
others, 41–43
excused absences, 8

Farrar, E., 79
Fine, M., 80
Finn, Jeremy, 12
Fogelman, 8
Foundations of Social Theory, 14

George W. Wingate High School, 10
getting caught: blanket, by gender,
31–32; by ethnicity, 43–44; by
grade level, 56–57; post-
registration, by gender, 32–33
Giuliani, Rudolf, 27

97

grade level and truancy, 10, 53–54; faking illnesses, 55–56; getting caught, 56–57; post-registration, 51–52; punishment, 59; reporting to parents, 58

Haller, E. J., 7
Hickerson, N., 79
Hirschman, A. O., 79

International Encyclopedia of Education, 8

Jessor, R., and S. L., 10
Jones, C., 10

Kaeser, S. C., 8
Kaplan, H. B., 7

Leithwood, K., 12
Levine, R., 13
listening to students, 79
Liu, X., 7

Moos, R. H., and B. S., 4, 7
Morgan, C., 11
Murgatroyd, S., 11

National Educational Longitudinal Studies–1988 (NELS:88), 5
Natriello, G., 3, 7–8, 75–76
Neill, A. S., 86
NELS:88. *See* National Educational Longitudinal Studies–1988
New York City, 78
New York Times, 9

O'Keeffe, D., 8–9, 17, 23, 26, 82, 85
one best system, 74

Paterson, F. M. S., 82
peer facilitator programs, 84
peer group, 12
post-registration, 9, 17, 23–25, 68, 78; getting caught, 57; by grade level, 51–52; by grades, 47–48; monitoring, 83; reducing, 82; by student attitudes, 69. *See also* truancy
Powell, A., 79
punishment for truancy, 13, 18, 22; by academic achievement, 50; by ethnicity, 45–46; by gender, 35–36; by grade level, 59
purposive action, 14

reporting truancy to parents, 22; by ethnicity, 44–45; by gender, 33–34; by grade level, 58
Risser, W., 7
Rubin, J. C., 27
ruralness, 7

Sarason, S., 80
school planning, 11
school size, 7
The Shopping Mall High School, 79
skipping. *See* post-registration
South Shore High School, 10
Stallings, Jane, 9
STAR. *See* Student Truancy and Attendance Review-II
Stoll, P., 8–9, 17, 23, 26, 82, 85
student attitudes, 62–64; academic progress, 63, 69–70; correlation analysis of, 65–68; extracurricular activities, 64; friends, 63; parental help, 63–64; reliability, 64; school, 64, 69; self-concept, 64; teachers, 63

Student Truancy and Attendance Review-II (STAR), 2, 18, 22, 39, 43, 63, 70, 78
Summerhill School, 86

Time, 27
Tobias, A., 84
Total Quality Management (TQM), 11
TQM. *See* Total Quality Management
Travis, J. E., 73
truancy: academic achievement and, 48–49, 68; academics and, 46–47, 63, 69–70; age distribution and, 20–21; as a universal behavior, 81; blanket, 17, 32, 68, 69; causes of, 11–13; characteristics of, 17, 19–20; collective action against, 18; complexities of, 3; definition of, 1; differentiations, 8, 82; encouraging, 7; enforcement against, 3; environment and, 18; extracurricular activities and, 75; faking illnesses and, 22, 39–40, 55–56; false causes of, 2; gender and, 10, 26–29, 31–36; "good" reasons for, 15; grades and, 4;

health and, 9; language and, 38–39; levels of, 22–23; myths of, 18; parents and, 84; predicting, 68–69; prosecuting, 77; rational choice of, 74; reducing, 85; school characteristics and, 21; school involvement and, 85; school recommendation and, 61–62, 68–69; school rules and, 60–61; sex. *See* truancy, gender; socioeconomic status and, 10; state funding and, 15; stricter teachers and, 13; student attitudes and, 69; teacher support and, 83; Web information on, 4; with others, 22, 30–31, 41–42; years in school and, 52–53. *See also* post registration.
truancy rates of: drop-outs, 5–6; seniors, 5–6
truant officer. *See* attendance director
Tulsa County, Oklahoma, 76–78
Tyack, David, 74

Wilce, H., 84
Wilson, K. G., 3, 76–78

Zuckerman, M., 12

About the Authors

Rita E. Guare, Ph.D., is an associate professor in the Division of Educational Leadership, Administration, and Policy (ELAP), at the Fordham University Graduate School of Education in New York City. In addition, she is president of the University Faculty Senate. Her doctorate is from Fordham, and she has taught at Fairfield University and Saint Joseph's College where her research interests are in philosophy and history of education. See her chapters, "Reclaiming Thoughtfulness and Imagination in Educational Leadership: A Moral Commitment to Enlightened Reason," in D. Jedan (Ed.), *Moral Philosophy and Education* (2001) and "Justice-seeking in History, Philosophy, and the Arts: The Legacy and Unfinished Agenda for Post Modern Educational Learders," in C. Lueth (Ed.), *Postmodern Philosophy and Education* (2002). More recently, her interests include ethics, spirituality, and the arts. See her work, "Jubilee Justice: Educating the Ethical Imagination through Literature," in P. M. Jenlink (Ed.), *Marching into a New Millennium: Challenges to Educational Leadership*, (ScarecrowEducation 2000); "The Power of Imagination: Spirituality and the Arts," in L. T. Fenwick (Ed.), *School Leadership: Expanding Horizons of the Mind and Spirit* (1999); and, "Educating in the Ways of the Spirit: Teaching and Leading Poetically, Prophetically, Powerfully," *Religious Education*, 96 (1) (Winter, 2001). As a high school assistant principal, dean, and then principal, her focus was on improving teaching-learning and encouraging interdisciplinary conversations. It was during her tenure in those positions that she became interested in truant behavior.

Bruce S. Cooper, Ph.D., is professor and vice chair, Division of Educational Leadership, Administration, and Policy (ELAP), at the Fordham University Graduate School of Education, in New York City. His Ph.D. is from the University of Chicago, and he has taught at University of Pennsylvania and Dartmouth College where his research includes the financing, equity, and budgeting of schools, and recently the abortive attempts of the National Education Association (NEA) and American Federation of Teachers (AFT) to merge into the United States's largest union. His research on school finance included work with Coopers and Lybrand on building a model that tracks resources to children in the classroom, and a new software produce, In$ite for schools. See his books, *Advocacy or Accuracy: The Politics of Research in Education Yearbook of the Politics of Education Asssociation* (1999) and *Optimizing Education Resources* (1998). Recent publications include *Promises and Perils Facing Today's School Superintendents* (ScarecrowEducation and AASA, 2003); "Urban Teachers Unions Face Their Future: The Dilemmas of Organizational Maturity," *Education and Urban Society*, 34:1, November 2001, pp. 101–118; "Advanced Budgeting Technology in Education: The Future Is Now," with Sheree T. Speakman, *School Business Affairs*, February 2001.